PA
3877   ARISTOPHANES
.R3   The frogs
1962

06074

Aristophanes

The Frogs

Translated by Richmond Lattimore
with sketches by Richard Sears

Ann Arbor

The University of Michigan Press

Published in the United States of America by
The University of Michigan Press and simultaneously
in Toronto, Canada, by Ambassador Books Limited

Library of Congress Catalog Card No. 62-7234

Manufactured in the United States of America
by The Haddon Craftsmen, Inc., Scranton, Pa.

Designed by George Lenox

CONTENTS

Introduction

The Frogs was produced at the Lenaia of 405 B.C. and won first prize.[1] The Athenians had been at war most of the time since 431 B.C., and their position now was almost desperate. Since the failure in Sicily, they had indeed won several naval battles and had twice been offered peace by Sparta; they were nevertheless in a position where one defeat would lose the war (this happened six months after The Frogs was presented). One great victory might still save them, but only if they used it wisely, as a bargaining point for permanent peace.

This, at least, seems to have been the view of Aristophanes. The champion of peace who spoke in The Acharnians, Peace, and Lysistrata, is still the champion of peace. It was Kleophon who had forbidden the Athenians to accept Spartan terms, and in this play Aristophanes hates Kleophon as much as ever. But peace cannot now be simply offered or accepted; it must be earned. Aristophanes' program can be summed up as "all hands save ship." All talents and resources, even the doubtful and suspect talents of Alkibiades, must be called on to win one more victory which, if won, must be used as a means to an honorable peace, not as a means to conquest and empire. So, at least, I would read the concluding lines of the play.

In the spring of 405, Athenian literature had suffered too. Aeschylus was dead half a century since, though not forgotten. Euripides and Sophocles, greatest of the moderns, had died within the year. Dionysos, masked though he may be as the preposterous hero of comedy, is also Drama, the spirit and essence of Athenian literature and art. He seeks to bring back good writing to Athens, and with it, the public wisdom which, as Aristophanes maintains against Sokrates, will always be found in the highest poetry.

The first part of The Frogs, therefore, takes the form of the Comic Journey beyond the limits of the world, reminiscent in some ways of Peace and The Birds. During its course, as the Dead are encountered,

---

[1] . . . "It was presented in the archonship of Kallias . . . at the Lenaia. It was placed first; Phrynichus was second with The Muses; Plato third, with Cleophon. Our play was so much admired because of the parabasis that it was actually given again, according to Dicaearchus." From the ancient Hypothesis, or Introduction. The Plato in question is a well-known comic poet, not the philosopher.

these are used to speak the poet's own views and to plead for political harmony. At the end of the Journey, a conversation between the two slaves, Xanthias and Aiakos, introduces the grand final *agon* between Euripides and Aeschylus.

This *agon* is, after suitable introductory exhortation and preparation, disputed on five issues, or in five rounds, as follows:
1. 907-1098. General style, subject matter, and effect upon audiences.
   (1099-1118). Choral interlude.
2. 1119-1250. Prologues, including skill at exposition and the use of iambic metre.
   (1251-60). Choral interlude.
3. 1261-1369. Lyrics and lyric prosody.
   (1370-77). Choral interlude.
4. 1378-1410. The weighing of lines.
   (1411-17). Interlude by Dionysos and Pluto.
5. 1417-65. Advice to the Athenians.

In each round, Euripides attacks first, and in the first three he scores some hits. Nor is his final advice (1446-50) contemptible; at least, it is not unlike the spirit of the poet's own views spoken at 718-37. But Aeschylus, the ultimate winner, has the better position for an *agon,* since the last word is always his.

Briefly, the arguments, round by round, are as follows:
1. Euripides says that Aeschylus is slow moving, undramatic, turgid, obscure, and too militaristic. His own plays are lucid, plausible, and have meaning for all. Aeschylus retorts that he has always maintained a high heroic standard and incited the citizens to virtue, while Euripides, in bringing Tragedy down to earth, has, especially with his morbid interest in sex, dragged her in the dust, and in so doing has unmanned the Athenians.
2. Euripides alleges an obscure and repetitious style. Aeschylus replies with a charge of metrical monotony. In prologue after prologue of Euripides, the main verb is delayed and a subordinate clause completed in such a way that the phrase
   lost his little bottle of oil
   which scans

   will now complete both the sentence and the metrical line.
3. Aeschylus having raised the question of metrical monotony, Euripides retorts in kind. The lyrics of Aeschylus are monoto-

nous. For, however he may begin, he constantly ends with the dactylic phrase

⏑ —◡◡ —◡◡ —◡◡ — —

exemplified by his line

> o ho what a stroke come you not to the rescue?

In these metrical criticisms, which are penetrating, the general criticisms of style are repeated, i.e., when Euripides makes sense, he is prosy and pedestrian, when Aeschylus sounds grand, he means little. Aeschylus counters. Euripides writes vers libre, the lyric metres lose their form and the sense loses its coherence. The result is a shoddy, sentimental, drifting sequence, marked in particular by one special fault which Aristophanes loves to detect in Euripides: namely, the unassimilating conjunction of magnificence and homeliness.

4. The weighing of the lines involves a bit of byplay, has been often dismissed as mere fooling, and is mostly that, but nevertheless forwards the constant opinion of Aristophanes (Dionysos): the verse of Aeschylus has more mass, heft, and force than that of Euripides.

5. What shall Athens do? The speakers might represent the poet's own agonizing struggle. Euripides expresses Aristophanes' doubts about the good purposes of the heirs of Perikles, the exponents of naval warfare; but Aeschylus voices Aristophanes' unwilling conclusion, that these men alone have a chance of saving the city.

In this *agon*, Aristophanes has achieved an unfair but telling criticism of Euripides. His Aeschylus, even as parody, fits far less closely the concept which we can form of him from seven complete plays and a number of fragments. Aeschylus was not the Colonel Blimp that Aristophanes makes him. *The Persians* and *The Seven Against Thebes* are not simple glorifications of patriotism and courage. *Agamemnon* condemns war-makers and sackers of cities. The woman's point of view is eloquently stated in every surviving play. And Aphrodite did mean a great deal to Aeschylus; one need only look at the dreaming visions of Helen in *Agamemnon*, or at Klytaimnestra's sadistic ecstasies in the same play. Nor was Aeschylus a reactionary aristocrat. *Prometheus* and *The Eumenides* speak eloquently for progress and reform.

Aristophanes has picked out and exaggerated certain aspects of Aeschylus, not because he was ignorant or blind, but perhaps because he was more concerned with the force of his *agon* than with the inward coherence and validity of his historical persons. The attack is on the moderns. Euripides is their spokesman. Whatever Euripides is, Aeschylus must be the opposite. So, if Euripides is pacific and unmilitary, Aeschylus must be martial. If Euripides is fascinated by the women and writes of their problems from their point of view, Aeschylus must despise sex. And since Euripides was so plainly popular (though not in the sense that he won prizes from the judges), Aeschylus must be in a sense *un*popular, that is, haughty and aristocratic.

A byproduct of the pattern is the unhappy position in which Sophocles finds himself: a second-best Aeschylus. Only two could play this game at once. Aeschylus and Euripides were plainly more fun for the parodist, their peculiarities being a great deal more obvious.

In translating *The Frogs,* I have found myself surprised into breaking away from several principles which I always stuck to when trying to translate serious Greek poetry. Let me, once again, grimly itemize.

1. Notes.   I have generally avoided footnotes on the text of tragedy. But Aristophanes is, as the immortal Stephen Leacock put it . . . "sally after sally, each sally explained in a footnote calling it a sally."[2] I have added some notes.

2. Slang.   The Frogs opens in the manner, though not altogether in the language, of the vaudeville act or minstrel show. My English is much worse than Aristophanes' Greek. But the vernacular seemed to be the only language into which it would translate itself. Frequently, the translation is in very bad taste. And so is Aristophanes.

3. Incongruity.   Comedy does not cultivate appropriateness for its own sake.

4. Rhymes.   Certain metres, such as short iambic lines, and the long ones in iambic and anapaestic, seemed in English to come out rather lame and labored without rhyme, perhaps because English lacks the flexibility and the bold distinction between long and short of polysyllabic Greek. I have left the parabasis (354-71) unrhymed because it seems, in Greek, rather strained and awkward, and is not funny.

Clichés.   In serious verse, these are absolutely obnoxious (in serious *prose,* too!). Awkwardly enthroned out of context, the cliché is of the stuff of comedy. So I have written accordingly. Perhaps the alert reader will find that they have crept into the introduction too.

I have used the *Oxford Classical Text* of Hall and Geldart.

I am deeply indebted to Harry Avery for helpful criticism.

---

[2] Let me point out that, in accordance with modern convention, this quotation from Stephen Leacock must be accompanied by a footnote calling it a quotation from Stephen Leacock. See Stephen Leacock, *Behind the Beyond* (New York: John Lane Company; London: John Lane, The Bodley Head; Toronto: Bell and Cockburn, 1923), pp. 186-87.

Characters in the Play

DIONYSOS

XANTHIAS, *his slave*

HERAKLES

CORPSE

CHARON

CHORUS *(as Frogs; as Initiates;*
and as the population of Hades)

AIAKOS, *the janitor of Hades*

MAID

HOSTESS *of the inn*

PLATHANE, *maid of the inn*

EURIPIDES

AESCHYLUS

PLUTO *(or Hades)*

VARIOUS EXTRAS *(stretcher bearers, dead souls rowing in the*
boat, assistants to Aiakos, etc.)

SCENE: *A Door. Enter Dionysos, on foot; Xanthias,*
riding a donkey, and with a bundle on his back.
Dionysos wears a long yellow robe, but over it the
lion skin affected by Herakles, and he carries a
primitive knobby club.

XANTHIAS
Shall I give them any of the usual jokes, master?
You know, the ones that are always good for a laugh?

DIONYSOS
Go ahead. *Any* of them. Except "what a day!"
Don't give them that one. It's gone awfully sour.

XANTHIAS
But something witty, like . . .

DIONYSOS
                        *A*nything. Except "my poor back."

XANTHIAS
Well, can I tell the really funny one?

DIONYSOS
                        Yes, do,
go right ahead. Only don't say *this* one.

XANTHIAS
                        Don't say what?

DIONYSOS
Don't shift your load because "you need to go to the baffroom."

XANTHIAS
Can't I even tell the people I'm so over-loaded
that unless somebody unloads me I'll blow my —— bottom?

DIONYSOS
No, don't, please don't. Wait till I *need* to vomit.

XANTHIAS
So what did I have to carry all this stuff for,
if I can't pull any of the jokes Phrynichos* pulls,
or what Lykis pulls, or what Ameipsias pulls?

DIONYSOS
Well, just don't do it. When I'm in the audience

7

and have to watch any of these conscious efforts,
I'm a year older when I leave the place.

XANTHIAS
Poor me. Oh, my poor neck. I think it's broken now.
It won't say anything funny.

DIONYSOS
Now isn't this a sassy slave? I've spoiled him.
Here am I, Dionysos, son of Grapejuice,
wearing out my own feet, and I let him ride
so that he won't get tired carrying the bundles.

XANTHIAS
What do you mean, not carrying them?

DIONYSOS
                              How can you?
You're riding.

XANTHIAS
            But I'm carrying.

DIONYSOS
                        How?

XANTHIAS
                        With an effort.

DIONYSOS
Isn't the donkey carrying what you're carrying?

XANTHIAS
Not carrying what I'm carrying, no, by golly.

DIONYSOS
How can you carry it, when somebody's carrying you?

XANTHIAS
Dunno. I only know my shoulder's falling apart.

DIONYSOS
All right, so the donkey isn't doing any good,
why don't you pick him up and carry him?

XANTHIAS
Why wasn't I in that sea battle,* where they freed the slaves
who fought? Then I could tell you to go jump in the lake.

DIONYSOS

Get down, you bum. Here we are at the door.
This is the place I was trying to find. First stop. Get down.

Knocks on the door.

Hey there! You inside! Hey. Anybody home? Bang bang.

Herakles half opens the door, pokes his head out.

HERAKLES

Who was pounding on my door? Sounded like a Centaur
kicking it or something. What goes on?

DIONYSOS

To Xanthias.

Slave boy!

XANTHIAS

What is it.

DIONYSOS

You noticed, didn't you?

XANTHIAS

Noticed what?

DIONYSOS

How scared he was.

XANTHIAS

Yeah, scared. Scared you were going bats.

HERAKLES

De*me*ter! I have to laugh.
I'm biting my lip to hold it in, but I can't help it.

DIONYSOS

Come here, dear boy. I have a favor to ask of you.

HERAKLES

Wait till I get rid of the giggles. Only I can't stop them.
That lion skin being worn over that buttercup nightie!
Haw haw haw.

Collapses. Recovers.

What's the idea, this meeting of the warclub and slipper?
Where were you bound?

DIONYSOS

Well, I served aboard a kind of dreamboat named the Kleisthenes.*

HERAKLES

And did you engage?

DIONYSOS

I did. We sank a dozen, a baker's dozen, of the enemy craft.

HERAKLES
You two?

DIONYSOS

So help me Apollo.

XANTHIAS

And then I woke up.

DIONYSOS
So then I'm sitting on deck, see, reading this new book: *Andromeda,* by Euripides: all of a sudden it hits me over the heart, a craving, you can't think how hard.

HERAKLES
A craving, huh, A big one?

DIONYSOS

Little one. Molon*-size.

HERAKLES
A craving. For a woman?

DIONYSOS

No.

HERAKLES

For a boy?

DIONYSOS

No no.

HERAKLES
For a, uh, man?

DIONYSOS

Shush shush shush.

11

HERAKLES

Well, what about you and
Kleisthenes?

DIONYSOS
Don't laugh at me, brother dear. Truly I am in a bad way.
I've got this craving. It's demoralizing me.

HERAKLES
What kind of craving, little brother?

DIONYSOS

I don't know how
to explain. I'll paraphrase it by a parable.
Did you ever feel a sudden longing for baked beans?

HERAKLES
Baked beans? Gosh yes, that's happened to me a million times.

DIONYSOS
Shall I give you another illustration? Expound this one?

HERAKLES
Don't need to expound baked beans to me. I get the point.

DIONYSOS
Well, that's the kind of craving that's been eating me:
a craving for Euripides.

HERAKLES
You mean, dead and all?

DIONYSOS
And nobody's going to persuade me to give up my plan
of going after him.

HERAKLES
Way to Hades', down below?

DIONYSOS
Absolutely. Belower than that, if there's anything there.

HERAKLES
What do you want?

DIONYSOS
What I want is a clever poet
*For some of them are gone. The ones who're left are bad.**

12

HERAKLES
What? Isn't Iophon* living?

DIONYSOS
He's the one good thing
that's left—that is, if he really is any good.
I don't quite altogether just know about that.

HERAKLES
But if you *got* to resurrect somebody, why
not Sophocles instead of Euripides?

DIONYSOS
No. First I want to get Iophon all by himself
without Sophocles, take him apart, see how he does.
Anyway, Euripides is a slippery character
who'd like to make a jailbreak and come back with me.
Sophocles behaved himself up here. He would down there.

HERAKLES
What happened to Agathon?*

DIONYSOS
Oh, he's left me, gone away.
And he was a good poet, too. His friends miss him.

HERAKLES
Too bad. Where did he go?

DIONYSOS
To join the saints. For dinner.

HERAKLES
What about Xenokles?

DIONYSOS
I only wish he *would* die.

HERAKLES
Pythangelos?

XANTHIAS
And nobody ever thinks of me,
and look at me standing here with my shoulder dropping off.

HERAKLES
Look here, there still are a million and one young guys around.

You know, Tragic Poets
who can outgabble Euripides by a country mile.

DIONYSOS
A lot of morning-glories talking to themselves,
just twitterbirds and free-verse writers, sloppy craftsmen.
One performance, and you never hear of them again.
They sprinkle Drama in passing like a dog at a pump.
You tell me where there's still an honest-to-god poet
to bark me out one good round solid tragic line.

HERAKLES
Honest-to-god like what?

DIONYSOS
                Honest-to-god like this,
someone with an adventurous style, as who should say:
Bright upper air, Zeus' penthouse* or *the foot of Time,*
or *heart that would not swear upon the holy things*
or *tongue that was forsworn when the heart knew it not.*

HERAKLES
You like that stuff?

DIONYSOS
                It's absolutely dreamy, man.

HERAKLES
It's bilge. It's awful. Nobody knows it better than you.

DIONYSOS
Rule not my mind. Thine own is thy mind. Rule thou it.*

HERAKLES
No, really, it does seem the most awful slop to me.

DIONYSOS
You stick to food.

XANTHIAS
                And nobody ever thinks of me.

DIONYSOS
Now, let you tell me why I'm here, wearing all this stuff
that makes me look like you. It's so you can tell me
about your friends who put you up when you went *there*

to fetch the Kerberos dog. Well, I could use some friends,
so tell me about them. Tell me the ports, the bakery shops,
whorehouses, parks and roadside rests, highways and springs,
the cities, boarding houses, and the best hotels
scarcest in bedbugs.

XANTHIAS

                Nobody ever thinks of me.

HERAKLES
You poor idiot. You're really going to try and get there?

DIONYSOS
No more of that stuff, please, just tell me about the roads,
and what's the quickest way to Hades' underhouse,
and don't make it a hot one. Not too cold either.

HERAKLES
Hm. What's my first recommendation? What indeed?
Well, here's a way. You need a footstool and a rope.
Go hang yourself.

DIONYSOS

            Stop stop. That's a stifling sort of way.

HERAKLES
Well, there's a short well-beaten path. *Well-beaten,* I say,
via mortar-and-pestle.

DIONYSOS

             That's hemlock you're talking about?

HERAKLES
Nothing else but.

DIONYSOS

           A chilly way. It makes me shiver.
Your shins go numb.

HERAKLES
Shall I tell you about a downhill road? It's good and quick.

DIONYSOS
That's what I'd like. I'm somebody who hates to walk.

HERAKLES
Well, take just a little walk down to the Potters' Quarter.

DIONYSOS

Yes.

HERAKLES

Climb up the tower, the high one.

DIONYSOS

What do I do then?

HERAKLES

Watch for the drop of the signal torch that starts the race,
and when they drop it, all the spectators around
will say "go!" You go, too.

DIONYSOS

Go where?

HERAKLES

Over the edge.

DIONYSOS

I'd smash my twin croquettes of brains.
No, I won't go that way of yours.

HERAKLES

What *do* you want?

DIONYSOS

The way you went, the deathless way.*

HERAKLES

It's a long voyage.
The first thing that you'll come to is a great swampy lake.
It's bottomless.

DIONYSOS

Well then, how do I get across?

HERAKLES

There's an ancient mariner with a little tiny boat.
He'll take you across. And you'll give him two bits* for it.

DIONYSOS

Oh, gee.
Those two bits. You can't ever get away from them.
How did they ever get here?

HERAKLES

Theseus* brought them along from
Athens.
After that, you'll see snakes, and armies of wild animals,
monsters.

DIONYSOS
Stop trying to scare me out of this.
You'll never stop me.

HERAKLES

Next comes a great sea of mud
and shitten springs eternal, and people stuck therein,
whoever did an injury to his guest or host,
debauched some child and picked its pockets in the process,
or beat his mother up, or broke his father's jaw,
or swore an oath and broke it,
or copied out a tragic speech of Morsimos.*

DIONYSOS
Don't stop. I've got another one to add to those.
Whoever learned the war-dance by Kinesias.*

HERAKLES
Next a sweet sound of flutes will come upon your ears,
and you'll see a lovely light like the sunlight here above,
myrtles, and solemn troops and sweet societies
of men and women, and an endless clapping of hands.

DIONYSOS
And who are they?

HERAKLES

The blessed, the Initiates.*

XANTHIAS
And I'm the donkey carrying mystic properties,
but I don't mean to keep them for the rest of time.

HERAKLES
Ask them. They'll tell you everything else you need,
for they live closest to the road you have to go.
Their habitation is by Pluto's doors.
So, good luck, little brother.

Herakles disappears, shutting the door.

DIONYSOS

                              Oh, the same to you!
Keep healthy. You there, Xanthias, pick the bundles up.

XANTHIAS

You mean, before I've put them down?

DIONYSOS

                                    Get a move on.

XANTHIAS

Oh please, please don't make me do it. Why don't you hire
one of these stiffs they're carrying out? There'll be one soon.

DIONYSOS

What if I can't get one?

XANTHIAS

                              Then I'll do it.

DIONYSOS

                                  Fair enough.
Look, here comes a corpse now being carried out.
Corpse is brought in on a stretcher.
        Hey! Hey, you there, the dead one. I'm talking to you.
        Want to carry some luggage to Hades?
Corpse sits up.

CORPSE

How much?

DIONYSOS

Showing his hand.

                     That much.

CORPSE

                       Give me two bucks*?

DIONYSOS

My god no, that's too much.
Corpse lies down again.

CORPSE

                   Keep carrying me, you guys.

DIONYSOS

Hey, what's the matter, wait, we've got to work this out.

18

CORPSE
Two bucks. Put up or shut up.

DIONYSOS
Make it one and a half.

CORPSE
I'd sooner come to life again.
Corpse is carried off.

XANTHIAS
Stuck up bastard, isn't he? The hell with him!
I'll take the baggage.

DIONYSOS
You are nature's nobleman.
Let's go catch a boat.

CHARON
Off stage.
Woo-oop! Coming alongside!

XANTHIAS
What's going on here?

DIONYSOS
What indeed. Oh, here, it's the lake
right where he said it would be, and now here comes the boat.
Charon, in a little boat (on wheels) is pushed in.

XANTHIAS
So help me Poseidon, so it is, and Charon too.

DIONYSOS
O carry me Charon o sweet chariot carry me home.*

CHARON
Who wants a cruise? Relaxation from business worries?
The Meadows of Forgetting, or Horsefeatherland?
To go to the Dogs? To go to the Birds? To go to Hell?

DIONYSOS
Me.

CHARON
Get aboard and shake a leg.

DIONYSOS

Where d'you think we're bound?
Strictly for the Birds?

CHARON

We sure are, with you aboard.
Get on, get on.

DIONYSOS

Here, boy!

CHARON

No, I won't take a slave.
Only a veteran of our hide-saving sea battle.*

XANTHIAS

I would have made it but I was sick. I had the pinkeye.

CHARON

Then you can just take a little walk around the lake.

XANTHIAS

Where shall I wait for you?

CHARON

By the Stone of Parching Thirst,*
at the pull-off.

DIONYSOS

Got it?

XANTHIAS

Oh, I've got it. Wish I were dead.
What kind of bad-luck-sign did I run into this morning?

*Xanthias trudges off, carrying the bundles. Dionysos
climbs, awkwardly, into the boat.*

CHARON

You, sit to your oar.

Dionysos sits on his oar.

Anyone else going? Hurry it up.

*A few Extras (the ones who carried the corpse),
get into the boat, each taking an oar.*

Hey, *you* there. What d'you think you're doing?

DIONYSOS

With dignity.

I am sitting

to my oar. Exactly what you told me to do.

CHARON

Rearranging him.

Well, sit *here,* fatso. Sit like this. Got it?

DIONYSOS

Okay.

CHARON

Now get your hands away and bring them back.

DIONYSOS

Okay.

CHARON

Stop being such an ass, will you? Bring your weight forward.
Get your back into it.

DIONYSOS

What do you want? I never rowed before.
I'm no Old Navy Man. I didn't make the First Crew.*
How'm I supposed to row?

CHARON

Easily. Just begin to do it,
and you'll get a pretty song to give you the time.

DIONYSOS

Who's singing?

CHARON

It's a swan song, but the swans are lovely frogs.

DIONYSOS

Go ahead.

Give me the stroke.

CHARON

OO-pah, oo-pah.

*If he cares to, Charon can go on doing this all
during the following chorus.*

21

The Chorus appears, in green masks and tights, as
Frogs. They are Frogs only in this rowing-scene.
They dance around the boat.

CHORUS

Brekekekex ko-ax ko-ax,
Brekekekex ko-ax ko-ax,
children of freshwater ponds and springs,
gather we all together now
and swell our lofty well-becroaken chorus,
ko-ax ko-ax

Dionysos' Nysos-song
we sing to the son of Zeus,
Dionysos-in-the-marshes,
when with morning-frog-in-the-throat
the hangover-haggard procession
staggers to the holy Pot-Feast through my dominion,
brekekekex ko-ax ko-ax.

DIONYSOS

I think that I'm beginning to fail,
I'm raising blisters on my tail,
ko-ax ko-ax, I think I am,
but possibly you don't care a damn.

CHORUS

Brekekekex ko-ax ko-ax.

DIONYSOS

I can't hear anything but ko-ax,
go 'way, I'd like to give you the axe.

CHORUS

Of course, you fool, you can't hear anything else,
for the sweet Muses have gifted me with their lyres,
and Pan the horned walker, voice of reed in the woods,
and lyric Apollo himself goes glad for my singing
when with the music of piping my lyrical
song is heard in the pondy waters.
Brekekekex ko-ax ko-ax.

DIONYSOS

My bloody blisters refuse to heal.
My anguished bottom's beginning to squeal.
When I bend over it joins the attack.

CHORUS
Brekekekex ko-ax ko-*ak.*

DIONYSOS
Oh ah ye songful tribe, will you
shut up?

CHORUS
Exactly what we won't do.
Longer stronger
sing in the sunny daytime
as we wriggle and dive in the marsh-
flowers blithe on the lily pads
and dive and duck as we sing,
and when Zeus makes it rain
in green escape to the deep
water our song still pulses
and bubbles up from below.

DIONYSOS
Brepepepeps ko-aps ko-aps
I'm picking the rhythm up from you chaps.

CHORUS
We're sorry for us if *you* join in.

DIONYSOS
I'm sorry for *me* if I begin
to split in two from bottom to chin.

CHORUS
Brekekekex ko-ax ko-ax.

DIONYSOS
And the hell with you. I don't *care* what you do.

CHORUS
Whatever you say we'll croak all day
as long as we're stout
and our throats hold out.

DIONYSOS
Brekekekex ko-ax ko-ax.
There, I can do it better than you.

CHORUS
No, *we* can do it better than *you.*

DIONYSOS

No, *I* can do it better than *you*.
I'll croak away
if it takes all day,
brekekekex ko-ax ko-ax,
and I'll croak you down in the grand climax
brekekekex ko-ax ko-ax.

Frogs slink away. Silence.

Ha ha. I knew I could beat you. You and your ko-ax!

CHARON

Easy, easy. Ship oars now. Coming alongside.
Everybody off. Pay your fare.

DIONYSOS

Two bits for you, my good man.

Charon with his boat is wheeled off.

Xanthias! Hey, Xanthias! Now where's he got to? Xanthias!

XANTHIAS

Off.

Yoo hoo!

DIONYSOS

This way. Over here.

Xanthias appears.

XANTHIAS

Why, hello, master.

DIONYSOS

What's over there?

XANTHIAS

A lot of mud and darkness.

DIONYSOS

Well, did you see those criminal types he was talking
about, the murderers and swindlers?

XANTHIAS

Haven't *you* seen them?

Dionysos stares at the audience and points rudely.

DIONYSOS
Oh, sure, now I know where to look. They're all out there.
Well, what do we do next?

XANTHIAS
I think we'd better get out of here.
This is the place he said the wild animals would be,
you know, those monsters he was talking about.

DIONYSOS
Oh, him.
He was just laying it on thick, trying to frighten me.
He knows what a fighting man I am, and it makes him jealous.
There's nobody who's quite as vain as Herakles.
I wish we could have met some terrifying thing,
you know, some ghastly struggle, to make the trip worth while.

XANTHIAS
You know, I think I do hear something moving around.

DIONYSOS
Wh wh which direction?

XANTHIAS
Right behind us.

DIONYSOS
Get behind.

XANTHIAS
No, it's in front of us now.

DIONYSOS
You better stay in front.

XANTHIAS
I see it. It's an animal—an enormous thing.

DIONYSOS
What does it look like?

XANTHIAS
Monster. It keeps changing shape.
Now it's a cow. Now it's a mule. Oh, now it's a girl,
whee-whew, what a beauty!

DIONYSOS

Let me at her. Where'd she go?

XANTHIAS

Too late. No girl any longer. She turned into a bitch.

DIONYSOS

It's Empousa.*

XANTHIAS

Whoever she is, she done caught fire.
Her face is burning.

DIONYSOS

Does she have one brazen leg?

XANTHIAS

She does, she does. The other one is made of dung.
I'm not lying.

DIONYSOS

Where can I run to?

XANTHIAS

Where can I?

DIONYSOS
To the priest of Dionysos sitting in the front row.
Save me, your reverence! We belong to the same lodge.

XANTHIAS
Lord Herakles, we're lost.

DIONYSOS

Dumb-bell, don't call me that.
Don't give away my name. *Please.*

XANTHIAS
Lord Dionysos then.

DIONYSOS

No no, that's even worse.
Go on the way you were going.

XANTHIAS

Here, master, over here.

DIONYSOS
Got something?

XANTHIAS
Don't be frightened, we've come out all right
and I can speak the line now that Hegelochos spoke:
*The storm is over, and the clam has stilled the waves.**
Empousa's gone.

DIONYSOS
You swear it's true?

XANTHIAS
So help me Zeus.

DIONYSOS
Swear it again.

XANTHIAS
So help me Zeus.

DIONYSOS
Swear.

XANTHIAS
Help me Zeus.

DIONYSOS
What a fright. I lost my pretty color when I saw her.

XANTHIAS
Our donkey got a fright too, so you're all in yellow.*

DIONYSOS
Now what did I ever do to have this happen to me?
Looking upward.
Which one of you gods must I hold responsible for this?

XANTHIAS
Bright upper air, Zeus' penthouse? Or *the foot of time?*
Flute within.

DIONYSOS
Hey, you.

XANTHIAS
What is it?

DIONYSOS

Did   you   hear?

XANTHIAS

Did I hear what?

DIONYSOS

Flutes being blown.

XANTHIAS

I heard them too, and there's a crackle
and smell of torches. Seems like it's mysteries going on.

DIONYSOS

Let's just quietly squat where we are, and listen in.

CHORUS

Off.

Iacchos Iacchos*
Iacchos o Iacchos.

XANTHIAS

That's what I thought it was, master. The Initiates.
Remember, he told us, their playground's hereabouts. They sing
the Iacchos song by that noted theologian, Diagoras.*

DIONYSOS

I think you're right, but still we'd better sit quiet here
until we find out just exactly what goes on.

CHORUS

In white, as Initiates.

Iacchos! Well beloved in these pastures o indwelling
Iacchos o Iacchos
come to me come with dance steps down the meadow
to your worshipping companions
with the fruited, the lifebursting,
the enmyrtled and enwreathed garland on your brows, and bold-footed
stamp out the sprightly measure
of the dancing that's your pleasure,
of the dancing full of graces, full of light and sweet and sacred
for your dedicated chosen ones.

XANTHIAS

Demeter's daughter, Persephone, holy lady and queen,
ineffable fragrance wafts upon me. Roasting pigs!*

DIONYSOS
If I promise you a handful of tripes, will you shut up?

CHORUS
Let flames fly as the torch tosses in hand's hold
Iacchos o Iacchos
star of fire in the high rites of the night time.
And the field shines in the torch light,
and the old men's knees are limber,
and they shake off aches and miseries
and the years of their antiquity drop from them
in the magical measure.
Oh, torch-in-hand-shining.
Iacchos go before us to the marsh flowers and the meadow
and the blest revel of dances.

*Parabasis. The Chorus advances down stage and
the leader addresses the audience directly.*

LEADER

All now must observe the sacred silence: we ban from our choruses
  any
whose brain cannot fathom the gist of our wit; whose hearts and
  feelings are dirty;
who never has witnessed and never partaken in genuine cult of the
  Muses,
who knows not the speech of bullgobble Kratinos,* who knows not
  the Bacchic fraternity,
who laughs at cheap jokes that should not have been made, who writes
  such stuff at the wrong time,
who stirs up sedition dissension and hate, who does not like the
  Athenians,
who hopes to make money out of our quarrels and lights them and
  fans them to fury,
who holds high office and then takes bribes when the city is tossed in
  the tempest,
who sells out a ship or a fort to the enemy, smuggling our secret
  intelligence
from Aigina over to Epidauros, like any goddam tax-collecting
Thorykion,* with the oarpads and sails and pitch that was meant for
  our navy,
who goes on his rounds and collects contributions to finance the
  enemy's war fleet,
who, humming his cyclical verses the while, uses Hekate's shrine as
  a backhouse,*

who gets up to speak in the public assembly and nibbles at the fees
   of the poets
just because they once made a fool of him in the plays that our
   fathers established.
Such men I forbid, and again I forbid, and again I forbid them a
   third time,
let them get up and go from our choral mysteries.

           All others, strike
   up the singing
and dance of our holy and nightlong revels befitting this solemn
   occasion.

CHORUS

Slowly.

Advance all now, firmly
into the flower strewn hollows
of meadow fields. Stamp strongly
and jeer and sneer
and mock and be outrageous.
For all are well stuffed full with food.

Advance advance, sing strongly
our Lady of Salvation
and march to match your singing.
She promises
to save our land in season
for all Thorykion can do.

LEADER

Come now and alter the tune of the song for the queen of the
   bountiful seasons;
sing loud, sing long, and dance to the song for Demeter our lady and
   goddess.

CHORUS
Demeter, mistress of grave and gay,
stand by now and help me win.
Protect this chorus. It is your own.
Let me in safety all this day
play on and do my dances.
Help me say what will make them grin.
Help me say what will make them think.

Help me say what will make me win
in your own festival today
and wear the victor's garland.

LEADER
Change the tune.
Sing to the pretty god of the time   summon him to join us.
We have a sacred way to go   and he goes with us.

CHORUS
Iacchos, well-beloved spirit of song, o be
my leader and march along with me
this holy way.
Bring me to Eleusis swift and musically.
To you I pray.
Iacchos lover of dancing help me on my way.

You split my shirt to make them laugh and boo.
You cut my cheap little shoes in two.
My rags flap on me.
You know how to make do.
Wartime economy.
Iacchos lover of dancing help me on my way.

I saw a sweet little girl in the crowd down there.
As she leaned forward, her dress, I swear,
bust open a trifle
and I was happy to stare
at a bosomy eyeful.
Iacchos lover of dancing help me on my way.

DIONYSOS
I've always been a fellow who's good
at follow-my-leader; I gladly would
go down and help you play with her.

XANTHIAS
                                    I would if I could.

CHORUS
Shall we now, all together
make fun of Archedemos?*
Seven years he tries to naturalize and still he hasn't made it.

Now he's a leading citizen
among the upworld corpses.
Nobody up there can claim a similar fame—for being a bastard.

And Kleisthenes,* they tell me,
sits mourning among the tombstones,
and tears the hair from his you-know-where, and batters his jawbones.

He was seen, in his usual posture
in tears for his vanished sweetheart—
the dear little friend (of his after-end) Sebinos of Anaphlystos.

And Kallias,* they say,
the son of Ponyplay,
wears a panoply and has gone to sea and the ships with a lionskin
    over his hips.

DIONYSOS
Can any of you guys tell
me where Pluto happens to dwell?
We're visiting firemen. Never been here before.

CHORUS
Stop bothering me so.
You haven't got far to go.
He lives right here. Walk up and knock at the door.

DIONYSOS
Boy! Pick up the stuff again.

XANTHIAS
What's the matter with this guy?
Pick up, pick up, it's nothing but pick up bundles.

CHORUS
Forward, now
to the goddess' sacred circle-dance to the grove that's in blossom
and play on the way for we belong to the company of the elect,
and I shall go where the girls go and I shall go with the women
who keep the nightlong rite of the goddess and carry their sacred
    torch.

Let us go where roses grow
and fields are in flower,
in the way that is ours alone,

playing our blessed play
which the prosperous Fates today
ordain for our playing.

On us alone the sun shines here
and the happy daylight,
for we are Initiates, we
treat honorably
all strangers who are here
and our own people.

The white-robed Chorus file off.

DIONYSOS

Well, tell me, how am I supposed to knock on the door?
How do the natives knock on doors in these here parts?

XANTHIAS

Stop dithering around. Take a good whack at it.
You wear the gear and spirit of Herakles. Act according.

DIONYSOS

Knocking.

Boy! Hey, boy.

AIAKOS*

Inside.

Who's out there?

DIONYSOS

The mighty Herakles.

AIAKOS

Still inside but he will appear later on.

You hoodlum; did you ever have a nerve,
you bastard, bastard plus, and bastard double-plus.
You were the one who dragged our Kerberos-dog away.
You choked him by the collar and made off with him,
and *I* was on duty. We've got a scissors-hold on *you*.
We've got the cliffs of blackheart Styx* all ready for you,
the blood-dripping rocks of Acheron to shove you off—
or maybe the bloodhounds sniff your trail by Kokytos.
Echidna, our pet hundred-headed viper, waits
to chew your gizzard, and Muraina, eel of hell
shall have your lungs to gnaw on, while your kidneys go
with all the rest of your innards and the bleeding bowels

to the Teithrasian gorgons. Oh, they'll rip you up.
They're straining at the leash. I'll let them loose on you.
Dionysos collapses, doubled up.

XANTHIAS
What's the matter?

DIONYSOS
                       I can't hold it. Is there a god in the house?

XANTHIAS
You clown. Don't disgrace us. Alley oop! On your feet
before somebody sees you.

DIONYSOS
                    But I feel so faint.
Be a good chap, put a wet sponge over my heart.

XANTHIAS
Here it is, you put it.

DIONYSOS
                 Where are we?
*Takes it, searches, and claps it over his lower
anatomy.*

XANTHIAS
                   O ye golden gods,
is that where you keep your heart?

DIONYSOS
                    You see, the poor little thing
got awfully frightened, so she crept down there to hide.

XANTHIAS
You're the worst coward of all gods and men.

DIONYSOS
                      Who, *me?*
Call *me* a coward? Didn't I ask you for a sponge?
Nobody else would have dared do that.

XANTHIAS
                   What would they have done?

DIONYSOS
Laid there and stunk, that's what a good coward would have done.
I got to my feet again. What's more, united I stand.

XANTHIAS
That's manliness, by Poseidon.

DIONYSOS
                         Goodness gracious yes.

Long pause.
He talked so loud and said such awful things. Weren't you
a little scared?

XANTHIAS
                  Hell no, I never gave it a thought.

DIONYSOS
Well, tell you what. You win. I guess you're the hero-boy.
So you be me. Here you are. Here's the club, here's
the lion's skin.

Exchange going on.
                  You're the guy with the fearless guts.
I'll be you, and take my turn with the duffel bags.

XANTHIAS
*I cannot but obey thee.** Gimme. Hurry it up.

Exchange completed. Xanthias parades the stage.
Hey, look at me, everybody. I'm Xanthierakles.
Now see if I'm a sissy, like you.

DIONYSOS
                         You look like someone
who came from the same ward—but got rode out on a rail.
Well, there's the baggage. Suppose I've got to carry it.

A maid comes out of the door, and squeals with joy.

MAID
Why, *Her*akles! Darling, it's you! Come on inside.
When the Mistress* heard you might be around, she put the buns
in the oven, and lit the stove, and put the pots of beans
to cook, and, oh yes, barbecued you a steer, whole,
and there'll be cakes and cookies too. So come on in.

XANTHIAS
Thanks, it's awfully kind of you, but . . .

MAID
                              Hear me, Apollo,
I simply won't let you go away. Let's see, we were fixing
some roast chickens, and she was toasting the salted nuts

and mixing the wine—vintage stuff. Here, take my hand
and follow me in.

XANTHIAS

Awfully nice, but . . .

MAID

Don't be so silly.
It's all yours, and I won't let you go. Oh, there's a flute-player-
girl waiting for you inside, she's lovely, and two or three
dancers, too, I believe.

XANTHIAS

What did you say? Dancing girls?

MAID

Pretty, just come to flower, all bathed and plucked for you.
Come on, come on, they were just putting the tables out,
and the cook was taking the hot dishes off the stove.

XANTHIAS

*Danc*ing girls! Dancing *girls!* Run on ahead, will you please
and tell those dancing girls of yours I'm coming right in.

Maid disappears.

Boy, you pick up the baggage there, and follow me.

DIONYSOS

Hey, wait a minute. You didn't think I was serious,
did you, when I got you up as Herakles, for fun?
Xanthias, will you kindly stop being such an ass?
Here's your baggage again. Take it. It's all yours.

*During the following dialogue, the Chorus come
back on. They are no longer Initiates specifically,
but simply represent an ideal audience, the population of Hades.*

XANTHIAS

What is this, anyway? Are you thinking of taking back
What you gave me?

DIONYSOS

I'm not thinking of it, I'm doing it.
Give me that lionskin.

XANTHIAS

Witnesses! Make a note! I'll sue!
I'm putting this in the hands of my—uh—gods.

DIONYSOS

What gods,
you stupid clown, thinking you could be Herakles
Alkmene's son, when you're human, and a slave at that.

XANTHIAS
Oh, the hell with it. Here, take it, take it.

Re-exchange.

Maybe, though,
if God so wills, you'll find you need me after all.

CHORUS
There's an *adaptable* guy.
Must have been in the navy.
He's been around. He'll never get drowned.
Always knows where the gravy
is. The ships on her beam,
he's on the side that's dry.
He's got supersensory vision
like our glorious politician
Theramenes.* Just call him galosh
or any old boot you can easily put
on either your right- or your left-hand foot.

DIONYSOS
Here's what would have been funny.
Picture it like this.
Here's Xanthias and his honey
ready to kiss.
But he needs to go. Here's me,
and I hold the pot for him, see?
I make a pass at the girl's—well
anyway, he's on to me,
so he hauls off and socks
me one in the teeth, and knocks
the spots out of Attic Tragedy.

Hostess comes out the door.

HOSTESS
Plathane! Plathane! Come out, come out. Here's that awful man!
Remember the one who came to our hotel one time
and ate up sixteen loaves of our bread?

Plathane, the maid, emerges.

39

PLATHANE

Heavens yes
it's him, it's him.

XANTHIAS

Somebody's going to be sor-ry.

HOSTESS
That wasn't all. He made away with twenty pounds
of roast beef too.

XANTHIAS

Somebody's going to get hu-urt.

HOSTESS
And a lot of garlic.

DIONYSOS

Woman, you're crazy in the head.
You don't know what you're talking about.

HOSTESS

I don't, don't I?
You thought I wouldn't know you in your tragic boots?
Well, what about it? I didn't even mention the herrings.

PLATHANE
You didn't even mention our poor white feta cheese.
He ate the lot, boxes and all.

HOSTESS
Then, when I asked him please if he would pay for it,
he just glared at me, fighting mad. He bellowed at me.

XANTHIAS
Yes, that's exactly like him. He always does like that.

HOSTESS
Pretended he was out of his mind, and pulled a sword.

PLATHANE
You poor thing, so he did.

HOSTESS

He frightened us girls so
we had to run away upstairs and hide.
He charged away. Took our rush mats along with him.

XANTHIAS
Yes, that's him all the way.

PLATHANE
                              Let's do something about it.

HOSTESS
Run and get us a dead Politician. Kleon* will do.

PLATHANE
Bring the whole subcommittee. Bring Hyperbolos.
We'll fix him, once for all.

HOSTESS
                         You horrid gourmet, you,
I'd like to take a rock to you and break those teeth
you ate me out of house and home with.

PLATHANE
                                   And I'd like
to throw you in the ditch they bury criminals in.

HOSTESS
I'd like to find that carving knife you used
to cut our sausages up—and carve your neck with it.

PLATHANE
I'll go get Kleon. If we ask him he'll come today
and pull the stuffings out of this guy, bit by bit.

Women rush off. Long pause.

DIONYSOS
Dear Xanthias. How I love him. Wonder if he knows it.

XANTHIAS
I know what you're thinking about. You stop right there.
I will *not* be Herakles again.

DIONYSOS
                         Sweet little Xanthias
say not so.

XANTHIAS
           Tell me, how can I be Herakles,
Alkmene's son, when I'm human, and a slave at that?

DIONYSOS
I know you're cross, my Xanthias. I don't blame you a bit.
You can even hit me if you want, I won't say a thing.
I tell you: If I ever make you change again
I hope to die, with my whole family: my wife:*
my kiddies:* throw in bleary Archedemos too.

XANTHIAS
I note your oath, and on these terms I will accept.

Re-exchange going on, Xanthias becoming Herakles.

CHORUS
Now you've got his costume on you.
Now you've got a reputation
to live up to. Better do
a transformation.
Remember the kind of god*
you're supposed to be.
Act accordingly
with masculinity.
Be rough and tough
or you'll be reduced to the bottom roost
and have to carry the stuff.

XANTHIAS
Gentlemen, you are not so
far off the mark, but, you know,
I thought of that too.
If it's anything bad this lovely lad
hands it to me: anything good
he'd take it back if he could.
I'll chew brave herbs* and I won't take fright,
so fight fight fight
for Xanthias. Yea!
And it's time for it, boys. I hear a noise.
The doors! Trouble coming this way.

*Aiakos rushes out, followed by two unprepossessing
assistants.*

AIAKOS
There's the dog-stealer. Get him, fellows, tie him up
and take him away. We'll fix him.

DIONYSOS

Somebody's going to be sor-ry.

*Xanthias waves the club of Herakles and holds
them off.*

XANTHIAS

The hell with you. Keep away from me.

AIAKOS

So you'll fight, will you?
Hey Ditylas hey Skeblyas hey Pardokos,
out here. Fight going on! Come along, give us a hand.

The reinforcements rush on.

DIONYSOS

Tut tut. Shocking, isn't it, the way this fellow
steals from you, then assaults you?

AIAKOS

He's too big for his boots.

DIONYSOS

Outrageous, shouldn't be allowed.

XANTHIAS

So help me Zeus
and hope to die if I ever was in this place before
or ever stole a hair's worth of goods that belonged to you.
Here, I'll make you a gentlemanly* proposition, my man.
Here's my slave-boy. Take him, put him to the torture;
then kill me, if you find I did anything wrong.

AIAKOS

What tortures?

XANTHIAS

Oh, try them all. Tie him on the ladder,
hang him up, beat him with a whip of bristles, take his skin off,
twist him on the rack, pour vinegar up his nose,
pile bricks on him. Just give him the works—only please excuse him
from anything gentle, like soft onion-whips, or leeks.*

AIAKOS

Why, fair enough. And if I hit your slave too hard
and cripple him—the damages will be paid to you.

44

XANTHIAS

Never mind paying me. Take him away and work on him.

AIAKOS

I'll do it right here, so he'll confess before your eyes.
Here, put that luggage down. Be quick about it. See that you don't
tell me any lies.

DIONYSOS

I protest. I'm warning everybody
not to torture me. I'm a god. If you touch me
you'll have yourself to blame.

AIAKOS

What are you talking about?

DIONYSOS

I am immortal Dionysos, son of Zeus.

Pointing to Xanthias.

And *he*'s the slave.

AIAKOS

You hear that?

XANTHIAS

Oh, I hear it. Sure.
That's all the better reason for him to get a whipping.
If he's really a god, he won't feel anything.

DIONYSOS

Well, you're claiming you're a god too. So what about it?
Shouldn't you get the same number of strokes as me?

XANTHIAS

That's fair enough too. Whip us both, and if you see
either of us paying any attention, or crying in pain
at what you're doing, you'll know that one isn't a god.

AIAKOS

You must be a gentleman. Can't be any doubt about it,
the way you love a trial scene. Well, strip, both of you.

Xanthias and Dionysos bare their backs.

XANTHIAS

How are you going to make this even?

AIAKOS

Picking up a whip.

Easy.

Hit one of you first and then the other, and so on.

XANTHIAS

Okay.

AIAKOS

Hitting him.

There!

XANTHIAS

And when you hit me, see if I move.

AIAKOS

I did hit you.

XANTHIAS

Like hell you did.

AIAKOS

Hm. Must have missed him.

Well, here goes for the other one.

Hits Dionysos.

DIONYSOS

When are you going to hit me?

AIAKOS

I did hit you already.

DIONYSOS

Oh? Why didn't I sneeze?

I do when I'm tickled.

AIAKOS

Dunno. Let's try this one again.

XANTHIAS

You supposed to be doing something?

Aiakos hits him.

Oh my gosh!

AIAKOS

My gosh?

That hurt, did it?

46

XANTHIAS

        Nyet. Just thought of something. Time for my feast at Diomeia,* and the enemy won't let us hold it.

AIAKOS

The man's too religious. Can't get to him. Try the other one.

Hits Dionysos.

DIONYSOS

Wahoo!

AIAKOS

        What's the matter?

DIONYSOS

                There go the cavalry. That's their call.

AIAKOS

But there're tears in your eyes.

DIONYSOS

              Got a whiff of their onion rations.

AIAKOS

Didn't feel anything?

DIONYSOS

          Nothing that would bother me.

Aiakos goes back to Xanthias.

AIAKOS

I'd better go back to this one and try again.

Hits Xanthias.

XANTHIAS

Owoo!

AIAKOS

        What's the matter?

Xanthias holds up his foot.

XANTHIAS

            Take this thing out, will you? Thorn.

AIAKOS

Where am I getting to? Try this other one again.

Hits Dionysos.

DIONYSOS
*Apollo who art lord of Delos and Pytho.**

XANTHIAS
That hurt him! Didn't you hear?

DIONYSOS
                              It did not. I was
simply going over a line of verse by Hipponax.

XANTHIAS
You aren't trying. Give him a good hard whack in the ribs.

AIAKOS
Thanks. Good idea. Here, turn your belly. That's the way.
Hits Dionysos in the belly.

DIONYSOS
Owoo Poseidon . . .
                         Somebody did get hurt that time.

DIONYSOS

Singing.

Who dost hold sway
over Aigaion's promontories,
*or in the depths of the sea's green waters.**

AIAKOS
Demeter. I can't tell
which of you two is a god. You'd better go on in.
The master will know who you are, anyway,
and Persephone the mistress. They're real gods, those two.

DIONYSOS

Struck.

You're absolutely right, only I wish you'd thought
of that first. Then you wouldn't have had to whack me.
The principals enter the door, leaving the stage to
the Chorus.

CHORUS
Muse of the holy choruses come to us, come, make all enjoy my
      music,
cast your eyes on this multitude of wits here seated
sharper than Kleophon,* that sharper, on whose no-spik-Athenian
      beak

mutters bad pidgin-Attic,
Thracian swallowbird he
perched on a barberry blackball bush
singing his mournful nightingale threnody, how he must hang, though
    the votes come out equal.

LEADER
It's the right and duty of our sacred chorus to determine
better courses for our city. Here's the first text of our sermon.
All the citizens should be equal, and their fears be taken away.*
All who once were tricked by Phrynichos, caught and held and led
    astray,
ought to be allowed to join the rest of us, who slipped away.
Amnesty. Let's all forgive them for mistakes made long ago.
Nobody in our community ought to lose his civic rights.
Isn't it unfair that, just for having been in one sea fight,
slaves should have Plataian status,* and be over men once free?
Please, I'm not against their freedom in itself. I quite agree.
They deserve it. That's the only thing you've done intelligently.
Still, there are those others, men who also often fought at sea,
by your side, whose fathers fought for us, akin by blood to you.
Let their one fault be forgotten. Let them know your mercy, too.
Oh, Athenians, wise beyond all other men, forget your rage;
any man who fights at sea beside us, let him be our friend,
take him as a citizen, honored kinsmen; let all hatred end.
Now our city fights the storm and struggles in the grip of the waves,
surely this is not the time for your old hard exclusive pride.
Some day, you'll regret it, if you leave unsaid the word that saves.

CHORUS
If I have true discrimination to judge a man and his sorrows to come,
not long will our current baboon be here to bother us.
That is little Kleigenes,*
cheapest of all the lords of the babble-whirlpool-bath where soap's
    without soda.
What they really use
is the clay of Kimolos.
He won't be around very long, and he knows it,
but he carries a club against robbers whenever he goes on one of his
    drunken strolls.

LEADER
We've been thinking much of late about the way the city treats
all the choicest souls among its citizens: it seems to be
like the recent coinage as compared with the old currency.*

We still have the ancient money: finest coins, I think, in Greece,
better than the coins of Asia; clink them, and they ring the bell,
truly fashioned, never phony, round and honest every piece.
Do we ever use it? We do not. We use this wretched brass,
last week's issue, badly minted, light and cheap and looks like hell.
Now compare the citizens. We have some stately gentlemen,
modest, anciently descended, proud and educated well
on the wrestling ground, men of distinction who have been to school.
These we outrage and reject, preferring any foreign fool,
redhead slave, or brassy clown or shyster. This is what we choose
to direct our city-immigrants. Once our city would not use
one of these as public scapegoat.* That was in the former days.
Now we love them. Think, you idiots. Turn about and change your
    ways.
Use our useful men. That will look best, in case of victory.
Hang we must, if we must hang; but let's hang from a handsome tree.
Cultured gentlemen should bear their sufferings with dignity.

Aiakos and Xanthias come out of the door.
Xanthias is in his slave's costume.

AIAKOS
This master of yours, by Zeus the savior, he's a man
of parts, a gentleman.

XANTHIAS
                    That's a logical conclusion
if trencherman plus wencherman means gentleman.

AIAKOS
But he didn't have you on the mat and beat you up
even when you said you were the master and he was the slave.

XANTHIAS
He'd have been sorry if he had.

AIAKOS
                        Good slavemanship
that. Well played. Exactly the way I like to do it.

XANTHIAS
Come again, please. You like what?

AIAKOS
                        Seeing myself in action
when *I* get off where he can't hear, and curse my master.

XANTHIAS
What about sneaking out of doors after a good beating
and muttering at your master?

AIAKOS
                                    I enjoy that too.

XANTHIAS
And poking into his business?

AIAKOS
                                    Can you think of anything nicer?

XANTHIAS
My brother, by Zeus! How about listening at the keyhole
when masters are gossiping?

AIAKOS
                                    Just about sends me crazy, man.

XANTHIAS
And spreading secrets you listened in on? Like that?

AIAKOS
                                                        Who, me?
That's more than crazy, bud, that's super crazy plus.

XANTHIAS
Phoebus Apollo! You're one of us. Give me the grip,
and kiss me, and let me kiss you, and then tell me, please,
in the name of Zeus-of-the-slaves, who wears his stripes with us,
what's all this racket and yelling and screaming? What goes on
inside?

AIAKOS
        One's Aeschylus and one's Euripides.

XANTHIAS
Aha!

AIAKOS
Oh, it's a big business, it's a big business:
great fight among the corpses: this high argument.

XANTHIAS
What's it all about?

AIAKOS
                    We have a local custom here,
sort of award for literature and humanities,
and the one who wins top rating in the work he does
gets to eat dinner in the capitol and sits
in a chair next to Pluto, see?

XANTHIAS
                              I see.

AIAKOS
That's until somebody else comes along who's better
at it than he is. Then he has to move over.

XANTHIAS
                                        I don't see
Aeschylus having anything to worry about.

AIAKOS
He held the Chair of Tragedy.
He was the best at writing them.

XANTHIAS
                              So who is now?

AIAKOS
Well, when Euripides came down, he exhibited
before the toughs, the sneak-thieves, and the pickpockets
and the safecrackers and the juvenile delinquents,
and there's a lot of that in Hades, and they listened
to his disputations and his wrigglings and his twists
and went crazy, and thought he was the cleverest writer.
That all went to his head, so he challenged for the chair
where Aeschylus was sitting.

XANTHIAS
                              Didn't they throw him out?

AIAKOS
They did not. The public cried out for a contest
to see which one really was better than the other.

XANTHIAS
You mean, the criminal public.

AIAKOS
                              Sure. They yelled to heaven.

52

XANTHIAS
But wasn't there anyone on the side of Aeschylus?

AIAKOS
Honesty's scarce. The same down here; the same up there.

XANTHIAS
Well, what's Pluto getting ready to do about it?

AIKOS
He's going to hold a contest, an event, that's what,
and judge their skills against each other.

XANTHIAS
                                                  But how come
Sophocles didn't make a bid for the Tragic Chair?

AIAKOS
He never even tried to. When he came down here,
he walked up to Aeschylus, kissed him, and shook hands with him,
and gave up his claim on the chair, in favor of Aeschylus.
His idea, Kleidemidas* was telling me,
was to sit on the bench as substitute. If Aeschylus wins,
he'll stay where he is; if Aeschylus loses, then he means
to fight for his own art against Euripides.

XANTHIAS
So the thing's coming off?

AIAKOS
                                        Zeus, yes, in just a little while,
and all the terrors of tragedy will be let loose.
They're going to have a scale to weigh the music on.

XANTHIAS
What's the idea of that? Short-changing tragedy?

AIAKOS
And they'll bring out their rulers and their angled rods,
and T-squares, the kind you fold.

XANTHIAS
                                              Bricklayers' reunion?

AIAKOS
Wedges and calipers. You see, Euripides says
you have to wring the gist from tragedy, word by word.

53

XANTHIAS

I guess all this is making Aeschylus pretty mad.

AIAKOS

He lowered his head and glared, like a bull on the charge.

XANTHIAS

Who's going to judge this?

AIAKOS   .

                    That was sort of difficult.
They found the intellectuals pretty hard to find.
Aeschylus didn't go down so well with the Athenians.

XANTHIAS

Maybe he noticed most of them were bank robbers.

AIAKOS

Besides, he thought it was pretty silly for anyone
but poets to judge poets. Then your master came
along, and they handed it to him. He knows technique.
We'd better go inside. When the masters get excited,
you know what happens: screams and yells of pain—from us.

Aiakos and Xanthias go in the door.

CHORUS

Fearful shall be the spleen now of Thundermutter withinside
when the riptooth-sharpening he sees of his multiloquacious
antagonist to encounter him. Then shall ensue dread
eyewhirl of fury.

Horse-encrested phrases shall shock in helmtossing combat,
chariots collide in whelm of wreckage and splinter-flown action,
warrior beating off brain-crafted warrior's
cavalried speeches.

Bristling the hairy mane on his neck of self-grown horsehair
bellowing he shall blast the bolts from compacted joinery
banging plank by plank nailed sections of verse in
stormburst gigantic.

Next, mouthforged tormenter of versification, the slim-shaped
tongue unraveling to champ on the bit of malignance
wickedly shall chip and chop at its tropes, much
labor of lungwork.

Enter from the door Aeschylus and Euripides,
Dionysos, (in his proper costume, without the gear
of Herakles or Xanthias), and Pluto. The poets
stand one on each side of the stage. Three chairs
are placed. Pluto sits in the middle, Dionysos on his
right, and the chair on his left is empty.

EURIPIDES
I won't give up the chair, so stop trying to tell me to.
I tell you, I'm a better poet than he is.

DIONYSOS
You heard him, Aeschylus. Don't you have anything to say?

EURIPIDES
He's always started with the line of scornful silence.
He used to do it in his plays, to mystify us.

DIONYSOS
Now take care, Aeschylus. Don't be overconfident.

EURIPIDES
I know this man. I've studied him for a long time.
His verse is fiercely made, all full of sound and fury,
language unbridled uncontrolled ungated-in
untalkable-around, bundles of blast and boast.

AESCHYLUS
Is that so, child of the goddess of the cabbage patch?*
You, you jabber-compiler, you dead-beat poet,
you rag-stitcher-together, you say this to me?
Say it again. You'll be sorry.

DIONYSOS
                    Now, Aeschylus, stop it.
Don't in your passion boil your mortal coils in oil.

AESCHYLUS
I won't stop, until I've demonstrated in detail
what kind of one-legged poet this is who talks so big.

DIONYSOS
Black rams, black rams, boys, run and bring us black rams, quick.
Sacrifice to the hurricane. It's on the way.

AESCHYLUS

Why, you compiler of Cretan solo-arias,
you fouled our art by staging indecent marriages.

DIONYSOS

Most honorable Aeschylus, please stop right there.
And as for you, my poor Euripides, if you
have any sense, you'll take yourself out of the storm's way
before the hail breaks on your head in lines of wrath
and knocks it open, and your—*Telephos* oozes out—
your brains, you know. Now, gently, gently, Aeschylus,
criticize, don't yell. It's not becoming for two poets
and gentlemen to squabble like two baker's wives.
You're crackling like an oak log that's been set ablaze.

EURIPIDES

I'm ready for him. Don't try to make me back down.
I'll bite before I'm bitten, if that's what he wants,
with lines, with music, the gut-strings of tragedy,
with my best plays, with *Peleus* and with *Aiolos,*
with *Melegros,* best of all, with *Telephos.*

DIONYSOS

All right, Aeschylus, tell us what you want to do.

AESCHYLUS

I would have preferred not to have the match down here.
It isn't fair. We don't start even.

DIONYSOS

                              What do you mean?

AESCHYLUS

I mean my poetry didn't die with me, but his
did die with him; so he'll have it here to quote. Still,
if this is your decision, then we'll have to do it.

DIONYSOS

All right, bring on the incense and the fire, while I
in the presence of these great intelligences pray
that I may judge this match most literarily.
You, chorus, meanwhile, sing an anthem to the Muses.

CHORUS

Daughters of Zeus, nine maidens immaculate,
Muses, patronesses of subtly spoken acute brains

of men, forgers of idiom, when to the contest they hasten, with care—
sharpened wrestling-hooks and holds for their disputations,
come, o Muses, to watch and bestow
potency on these mouths of magnificence,
figures and jigsaw patterns of words.
Now the great test of artistic ability goes into action.

DIONYSOS
Both of you two pray also, before you speak your lines.

AESCHYLUS
Putting incense on the fire.
Demeter, mistress, nurse of my intelligence,
grant me that I be worthy of thy mysteries.

DIONYSOS
Now you put your incense on, too.

EURIPIDES
                              Excuse me, please.
Quite other are the gods to whom I sacrifice.

DIONYSOS
You mean, you have private gods? New currency?

EURIPIDES
                                        Yes, I have.

DIONYSOS
Go ahead, then sacrifice to your private gods.

EURIPIDES
Bright upper air, my foodage! Socket of the tongue!
Oh, comprehension, sensory nostrils, oh
grant I be critical in all my arguments.

CHORUS
We're all eager to listen
to the two great wits debating
and stating
the luminous course of their wissen-
schaft. Speech bitter and wild,
tough hearts, nothing mild.
Neither is dull.
From one we'll get witty designs
polished and filed.

The other can pull
up trees by the roots for his use,
goes wild, cuts loose
stampedes of lines.

DIONYSOS
Get on with it, get on with it, and put your finest wit in all
you say, and be concrete, and be exact; and, be original.

EURIPIDES
I'll make my self-analysis a later ceremony
after having demonstrated that my rival is a phony.
His audience was a lot of louts and Phrynichus* was all they knew.
He gypped and cheated them with ease, and here's one thing he used
  to do.
He'd start with one veiled bundled muffled character plunked down
  in place,
Achilleus,* like, or Niobe, but nobody could see its face.
It looked like drama, sure, but not one syllable would it mutter.

DIONYSOS
By Jove, they didn't, and that's a fact.

EURIPIDES
                              The chorus then would utter
four huge concatenations of verse. The characters just sat there mum.

DIONYSOS
You know, I liked them quiet like that. I'd rather have them deaf and
  dumb
than yak yak yak the way they do.

EURIPIDES
                              That's because you're an idiot too.

DIONYSOS
Oh, by all means, and to be sure, and what was Aeschylus trying to do?

EURIPIDES
Phony effects. The audience sat and watched the panorama
breathlessly. *"When will Niobe speak?"* And that was half the drama.

DIONYSOS
It's the old shell game. I've been had. Aeschylus, why this agitation?
You're looking cross and at a loss.

EURIPIDES

He doesn't like investigation.
Then after a lot of stuff like this, and now the play was half-way
   through,
the character would grunt and moo a dozen cow-sized lines or two,
with beetling brows and hairy crests like voodoo goblins all got up,
incomprehensible, of course.

AESCHYLUS

You're killing me.

DIONYSOS

Will you shut up?

EURIPIDES

Not one word you could understand . . .

DIONYSOS

No, Aeschylus, don't grind
   your teeth . . .

EURIPIDES

. . . but battles of Skamandros, barbicans with ditches underneath,
and hooknosed eagles bronze-enwrought on shields, verse armed like
   infantry,
not altogether easy to make out the sense.

DIONYSOS

You're telling me?
Many a night I've lain awake and puzzled on a single word.
A fulvid roosterhorse is please exactly just what kind of bird?

AESCHYLUS

It was a symbol painted on the galleys, you illiterate block.

DIONYSOS

I thought it was Eryxis, our Philoxenos's fighting-cock.

EURIPIDES

Well, should a rooster—vulgah bird!—get into tragedy at all?

AESCHYLUS

Tell me of *your* creations, you free-thinker, if you have the gall.

EURIPIDES

No roosterhorses, bullmoosegoats, nor any of the millions
of monsters that the Medes and Persians paint on their pavilions.

When I took over our craft from you, I instantly became aware
that she was gassy from being stuffed with heavy text and noisy air,
so I eased her aches and reduced the swelling and took away the
    weights and heats
with neat conceits and tripping feets, with parsnips, radishes, and
    beets.
I gave her mashed and predigested baby-food strained from my books,
then fed her on solo-arias.

DIONYSOS

             Kephisophon* had you in his hooks.

EURIPIDES

My openings were never confused or pitched at random. They were
    not
difficult. My first character would give the background of the plot
at once.

DIONYSOS

        That's better than giving away your personal background, eh,
  what, what?

EURIPIDES

Then, from the opening lines, no person ever was left with nothing to
    do.
They all stepped up to speak their piece, the mistress spoke, the slave
    spoke too,
the master spoke, the daughter spoke, and grandma spoke.

AESCHYLUS

                        And tell me
  why
you shouldn't be hanged for daring that.

EURIPIDES

                  No, cross my heart and hope
  to die,
I made the drama *democratic*.

DIONYSOS

To Aeschylus.

            You'd better let that one pass, old sport;
you never were such a shining light in that particular line of thought.*

EURIPIDES

Then I taught natural conversational dialogue.

AESCHYLUS

I'll say you did.
And before you ever taught them that, I wish you could have split in
   middle.

EURIPIDES

Going right on.

Taught them delicate tests and verbalized commensuration,
and squint and fraud and guess and god and loving application,
and always how to think the worst of everything.

AESCHYLUS

So I believe.

EURIPIDES

I staged the life of everyday, the way we live. I couldn't deceive
my audience with the sort of stuff they knew as much about as I.
They would have spotted me right away. I played it straight and
   didn't try
to bind a verbal spell and hypnotize and lead them by the nose
with Memnons and with Kyknoses with rings on their fingers and bells
   on their toes.
Judge both of us by our influence on followers. Give him Manes,
Phormisios* and Megainetos and sundry creeps and zanies,
the big moustachio bugleboys, the pinetreebenders twelve feet high,
but Kleitophon is mine, and so's Theramenes, a clever guy.

DIONYSOS

I'll grant your Theramenes. Falls in a puddle and comes out dry.
The man is quick and very slick, a true Euripidean.
When Chians are in trouble he's no Chian, he's a Keian.

EURIPIDES

So that's what my plays are about,
and these are my contributions,
and I turn everything inside out
looking for new solutions
to the problems of today,
always critical, giving
suggestions for gracious living,
and they come away from seeing a play
in a questioning mood, with "where are we at?,"
and "who's got my this?," and "who took my that?."

DIONYSOS

So now the Athenian hears a pome
of yours, and watch him come stomping home
to yell at his servants every one:
"where oh where are my pitchers gone?—
where is the maid who hath betrayed
my heads of fish to the garbage trade?
Where are the pots of yesteryear?
Where's the garlic of yesterday?
Who hath ravished my oil away?"
Formerly they sat like hicks
fresh out of the sticks
with their jaws hung down in a witless way.

CHORUS

To Aeschylus.

See you this, glorious
*Achilleus?** What have you got to say?
Don't let your rage
sweep you away,
or you'll never be victorious.
This cynical sage
hits hard. Mind the controls.
Don't lead with your chin.
Take skysails in.
Scud under bare poles.
Easy now. Keep him full in your sights.
When the wind falls, watch him,
then catch him
dead to rights.

DIONYSOS

O mighty-mouthed inventor of harmonies, grand old bulwark of
    balderdash,
frontispiece of Hellenic tragedy, open the faucets and let 'er splash.

AESCHYLUS

The whole business gives me a pain in the middle, my rage and
    resentment are heated
at the idea of having to argue with *him.* But so he can't say I'm
    defeated,
here, answer me, you. What's the poet's duty, and why is the poet
    respected?

EURIPIDES

Because he can write, and because he can think, but mostly because he's injected
some virtue into the body politic.

AESCHYLUS

What if you've broken your trust,
and corrupted good sound right-thinking people and filled them with treacherous lust?
If poets do that, what reward should they get?

DIONYSOS

The axe. That's what
we should do with 'em.

AESCHYLUS

Then think of the people *I* gave him, and think of the people when he got through with 'em.
I left him a lot of heroic six-footers, a grand generation of heroes,
unlike our new crop of street-corner loafers and gangsters and decadent queer-os.
Mine snorted the spirit of spears and splendor, of white-plumed helmets and stricken fields,
of warrior heroes in shining armor and greaves and sevenfold-oxhide shields.

DIONYSOS

And that's a disease that never dies out. The munition-makers will kill me.

EURIPIDES

Just what did you do to make them so noble? Is that what you're trying to tell me?

DIONYSOS

Well, answer him, Aeschylus, don't withdraw into injured dignity. That don't go.

AESCHYLUS

I made them a martial drama.

DIONYSOS

Which?

AESCHYLUS

Seven Against Thebes, if you
want to know.
Any man in an audience sitting through that would aspire to heroic
endeavor.

DIONYSOS

That was a mistake, man. Why did you make the Thebans more
warlike than ever
and harder to fight with? By every right it should mean a good beating
for you.

AESCHYLUS

To the audience.

Well, *you* could have practiced austerity too. It's exactly what *you*
wouldn't *do.*
Then I put on my *Persians,** and anyone witnessing that would
promptly be smitten
with longing for victory over the enemy. Best play I ever have written.

DIONYSOS

Oh, yes, I loved that, and I thrilled where I sat when I heard old
Dareios was dead
and the chorus cried "wahoo" and clapped with their hands. I tell you,
it went to my head.

AESCHYLUS

There, there is work for poets who also are MEN. From the earliest
times
incitement to virtue and useful knowledge have come from the
makers of rhymes.
There was Orpheus first. He preached against murder, and showed
us the heavenly way.
Musaeus taught divination and medicine; Hesiod, the day-after-day
cultivation of fields, the seasons, and plowings. Then Homer, divinely
inspired,
is a source of indoctrination to virtue. Why else is he justly admired
than for teaching how heroes armed them for battle?

DIONYSOS

He didn't teach
Pantakles, though.
He can't get it right. I watched him last night. He was called to
parade, don't you know,

and he put on his helmet and tried to tie on the plume when the helm was on top of his head.

AESCHYLUS

Ah, many have been my heroic disciples; the last of them, Lamachos (recently dead).
The man in the street simply has to catch something from all my heroics and braveries.
My Teucers and lion-hearted Patrokloses lift him right out of his knaveries
and make him thrill to the glory of war and spring to the sound of the trumpet.
But I never regaled you with Phaidra* the floozie—or Sthenoboia* the strumpet.
I think I can say that a lovesick woman has never been pictured by me.

EURIPIDES

Aphrodite never did notice you much.

AESCHYLUS

Aphrodite can go climb a tree.
But you'll never have to complain that she didn't bestow her attentions on you.
She got you in person, didn't she?

DIONYSOS

Yes, she did, and your stories came true.
The fictitious chickens came home to roost.

EURIPIDES

But tell me, o man without pity:
suppose I did write about Sthenoboia. What harm has she done to our city?

AESCHYLUS

Bellerophon-intrigues, as given by you, have caused the respectable wives
of respectable men, in shame and confusion, to do away with their lives.

EURIPIDES

But isn't my story of Phaidra a story that really has happened?

AESCHYLUS

So be it.

It's true. But the poet should cover up scandal, and not let anyone see it.

He shouldn't exhibit it out on the stage. For the little boys have their teachers

to show them example, but when they grow up we poets must act as their preachers,

and what we preach should be useful and good.

EURIPIDES

But you, with your massive construction,

huge words and mountainous phrases, is that what you call useful instruction?

You ought to make people talk like people.

AESCHYLUS

Your folksy style's for the birds.

For magnificent thoughts and magnificent fancies, we must have magnificent words.

It's appropriate too for the demigods of heroic times to talk bigger

than we. It goes with their representation as grander in costume and figure.

I set them a standard of purity. You've corrupted it.

EURIPIDES

How did I do it?

AESCHYLUS

By showing a royal man in a costume of rags, with his skin showing through it.

You played on emotions.

EURIPIDES

But why should it be so wrong to awaken their pity?

AESCHYLUS

The rich men won't contribute for warships.* You can't find one in the city

who's willing to give. He appears in his rags, and howls, and complains that he's broke.

68

DIONYSOS

But he always has soft and expensive underwear under the beggar-
man's cloak.
The liar's so rich and he eats so much that he has to feed some to the
fishes.

AESCHYLUS

You've taught the young man to be disputatious. Each argues as
long as he wishes.
You've emptied the wrestling yards of wrestlers. They all sit around
on their fannies
and listen to adolescent debates. The sailormen gossip like grannies
and question their officers' orders. In my time, all that they knew
how to do
was to holler for rations, and sing "yeo-ho," and row, with the rest
of the crew.

DIONYSOS

And blast in the face of the man behind, that's another thing too
that they knew how to do.
And how to steal from the mess at sea, and how to be robbers ashore.
But now they argue their orders. We just can't send them to sea any
more.

AESCHYLUS

That's what he's begun. What hasn't he done?
His nurses go propositioning others.
His heroines have their babies in church
or sleep with their brothers
or go around murmuring: "Is life life?"*
So our city is rife
with the clerk and the jerk,
the altar-baboon, the political ape,
and our physical fitness is now a disgrace
with nobody in shape
to carry a torch in a race.

DIONYSOS

By Zeus, you're right. I laughed till I cried
at the Panathenaia* a while ago,
as the torch-relay-runners went by.
Here comes this guy;
he was puffed, he was slow,
he was white, he was fat,
he was left behind,

and he didn't know where he was at,
and the pottery works gang
stood at the gates to give him a bang
in the gut and the groin and the ribs and the rump
till the poor fellow, harried
by one cruel thump
exploded his inward air
and blew out the flare that he carried.

CHORUS
Great is this action, bitter the spite, the situation is ripe for war.
How shall the onlooker judge between them?
One is a wrestler strong and rough;
quick the other one, deft in defensive throws and the back-heel stuff.
Up from your places! Into the ring again!
Wit must wrestle wit once more in fall upon fall.
Fight him, wrestle him, throw the book at him,
talk at him, sit on him, skin him alive,
old tricks, new tricks, give him the works.
This is the great debate for the championship. Hazard all.

Never hold back any attack for fear you may not be understood.
You have an audience who can follow you,
don't be afraid of being too difficult.
That could once have happened, but now we've changed all that.
   They're good
and they're armed for action. Everyone's holding
his little book, so he can follow the subtle allusions.*
Athenian playgoers, best in the world,
bright and sharp and ready for games
waiting for you to begin.
Here's your sophisticated audience. Play it to win.

EURIPIDES
All right, I'll work on your prologues first of all, because
they come at the beginning of every tragedy.
I'll analyse this great man's prologues. Did you know
how murky you were in getting your action under way?

DIONYSOS
How are you going to analyse them?

EURIPIDES
                              Lots of ways.
First, read me the beginning of your *Oresteia*.*

DIONYSOS
Silence all. Let no man speak. Aeschylus, read.

AESCHYLUS
Hermes, lord of the dead, who watch over the powers
of my father, be my savior and stand by my claim.
*I have come back to my own soil. I have returned.**

DIONYSOS
Find any mistakes there?

EURIPIDES
                              Yes, a dozen. Maybe more.

DIONYSOS
Why, man, the whole passage is only three lines.

EURIPIDES
But each of them has twenty things wrong with it.

Aeschylus growls.

DIONYSOS
Aeschylus, as counsel I advise you: keep quiet,
or you'll be mulcted, three lines of blank verse, plus costs.

AESCHYLUS
I have to keep quiet for *him?*

DIONYSOS
                              That's my advice to you.

EURIPIDES
He made one colossal howler, right at the beginning.

AESCHYLUS
To Dionysos

Hear that? *You*'re crazy.

DIONYSOS
                              Fact has never bothered me much.

AESCHYLUS
What kind of mistake?

EURIPIDES
                              Take it again from the beginning.

AESCHYLUS
Hermes, lord of the dead, who watch over the powers

EURIPIDES
Well, look, you've got Orestes saying this over the tomb
of his father, and his father's dead. That right?

AESCHYLUS
                                                That's right.

EURIPIDES
Let's get this straight. Here is where his father was killed,
murdered in fact, by his own wife, in a treacherous plot.
You make him say Hermes is *watching over* this.

AESCHYLUS
I don't mean the Hermes you mean. He was talking to
the Kindly Hermes of the world below. He made that clear
when he said he was keeping his inheritance for him.

EURIPIDES
Why that's a bigger and better blunder than I hoped.
It makes his inheritance an underworld property.

DIONYSOS
Orestes then would have to rob his father's grave?

AESCHYLUS
Dionysos, the wine you're drinking has bouquet. It stinks.

DIONYSOS
Read the next line. Watch for errors, Euripides.

AESCHYLUS
of my father, be my savior and stand by my claim.
I have come back to my own soil. I have returned.

EURIPIDES
Ha! The great Aeschylus has said the same thing twice.

DIONYSOS
Twice,   how?

EURIPIDES
                    Look at the sentence. Or better, I'll show you.
I have come back, he says, but also *I have returned.*
I have come back means the same as *I have returned.*

DIONYSOS
You're right, by golly. It's like saying to your neighbor:
"Lend me your kneading-trough, your trough to knead things in."

AESCHYLUS
You two jabberwocks, it is not the same thing at all.
The diction's excellent.

EURIPIDES
Show me. Tell me what you mean, will you, please.

AESCHYLUS
Come back just means getting back home again, arrival
without further context. If he gets there, he arrives.
The exile arriving *comes back;* but he also *returns*.

DIONYSOS
That's good, by god. What do you say, Euripides?

EURIPIDES
I say Orestes didn't *return,* if *returned* means
restored. It wasn't formal. He sneaked past the guards.

DIONYSOS
By god, that's good. (Except I don't know what you mean.)

EURIPIDES
Go on. Next line.

DIONYSOS
                    Yes, Aeschylus, better go on.
Keep at it. You, keep watching for anything wrong.

AESCHYLUS
*And by this mounded gravebank I invoke my sire
to hear, to listen. . . .*

EURIPIDES
                    Saying the same thing twice again.
To hear, to listen. Same thing twice. Perfectly clear.

DIONYSOS
Of course, you fool, he has to; he's talking to the dead.
We call to them three times,* and still we don't get through.

AESCHYLUS
How do you make *your* prologues, then?

EURIPIDES

                                        I'll give you some,
and if you catch me saying the same thing twice, or padding
my lines, without adding to the sense—spit in my eye.

DIONYSOS

Speak us some lines then, speak them. There's nothing else for it
than to listen to your prologues and criticize the verse.

EURIPIDES

*Oedipus at the outset was a fortunate man . . .**

AESCHYLUS

By god, he was not. He was most *un*fortunate
from birth. Before birth, since Apollo prophesied
before he was even begotten, that he would kill his father.
How could he have been, at the outset, *fortunate?*

EURIPIDES

. . . But then he became the wretchedest of humankind.

AESCHYLUS

He didn't *become* the wretchedest. He never stopped.
Look here. First thing that happened after he was born
they put him in a broken pot and laid him out in the snow
so he'd never grow up to be his father's murderer.
Then he went to Polybus, with sore feet, wasn't that luck?
and then he married an old lady, though he was young,
and also the old lady turned out to be his mother,
and then he blinded himself . . .

DIONYSOS

                              That would have saved his life
if he'd been a general along with Erasinides.*

EURIPIDES

You're crazy. The prologues that I write are very fine.

AESCHYLUS

By Zeus! I'm not going to savor you, word by word
and line by line, like you, but, with the help of the gods,
I'll ruin your prologues with a little bottle of oil.

EURIPIDES

Ruin my prologues with a bottle of oil?

AESCHYLUS

Just one
bundle of fleece or *bottle of oil* or *packet of goods.*
The way you write iambics, always there's just room
for a phrase the length of one of those. I'll demonstrate.

EURIPIDES
Demonstrate? Poof.

AESCHYLUS

I say I can.

DIONYSOS

Read us a line.

EURIPIDES
Aigyptos, as the common tale disseminates,
with all his sea-armada and his fifty sons
*coming to Argos**

AESCHYLUS

lost his little bottle of oil.*

DIONYSOS
A naughty little bottle. It'll be spanked for that.
Give us another line, I want to see what happens.

EURIPIDES
Dionysos, who, with thrysos and in hides of fawns
appareled on Parnassos up among the pines
*dances on light feet**

AESCHYLUS

lost his little bottle of oil.

DIONYSOS
*Ah me, again, I am struck again,** with a bottle of oil.

EURIPIDES
He hasn't done much to me; here's another prologue
I'll give him, where he can't tag on his bottle of oil.
There's been no man who's had good fortune all his days.
For one was born to fortune, but his goods are gone.
*One, born unhappy**

AESCHYLUS

lost his little bottle of oil.

DIONYSOS
Euripides.

EURIPIDES
    What?

DIONYSOS
               Maybe you'd better strike your sails.
That little bottle of oil is blowing up a storm.

EURIPIDES
Demeter be my witness, it doesn't mean a thing.
Here comes a line to smash his little—uh—property.

DIONYSOS
Go ahead, read another, but look out for that bottle.

EURIPIDES
Kadmos, son of Agenor, once upon a time
sailing from Sidon*

AESCHYLUS
              lost his little bottle of oil.

DIONYSOS
My poor dear friend, you'd better buy that bottle of oil
or it'll chew up all our prologues.

EURIPIDES
                  You mean that?
You're saying *I* should buy from *him?*

DIONYSOS
                  That's my advice.

EURIPIDES
I refuse to do it. I have lots of prologues left
where he can't tag on any little bottle of oil.
Pelops the son of Tantalos reaching Pisa plain
with his swift horses*

AESCHYLUS
              lost his little bottle of oil.

DIONYSOS
You see? Once more he makes the little bottle fit.
Now be a good fellow. It isn't too late yet, buy one quick.
For only a quarter you can get one, nice and new.

EURIPIDES

Not yet, by god, not yet. I still have plenty left.
*Oineus, from his land**

AESCHYLUS

lost his little bottle of oil.

EURIPIDES

Hey, wait a minute. Let me get a whole line out.
*Oineus from his land choosing out a store of grain
and sacrificing*

AESCHYLUS

lost his little bottle of oil.

DIONYSOS

In the middle of his sacrifice? Who found it for him?

EURIPIDES

Let me alone, please. See what he can say to this:
*Zeus, as the most authentic version hath maintained . . .**

DIONYSOS

He'll do you in. Zeus lost his little bottle of oil.
That bottle of oil is in your prologues everywhere
and multiplies like scabs of sickness in the eyes.
For god's sake, change the subject to his lyric lines.

EURIPIDES

Good idea. I've plenty of material to show
he's a bad lyric poet. It all sounds alike.

CHORUS

What can be the meaning of that?
Think as I will, I can not conceive
any thing he can say
against the man who can boast
the loveliest lyrics and the most
of any until today.
Much I wonder, what charge he can make
good against the great master
of tragic verse. He courts disaster.
I fear for his sake.

EURIPIDES

Wonder is right, if you mean his prosody. You'll see.
One little cut, and his metres all come out the same.

DIONYSOS

The same? Give me a handful of pebbles. I'll keep count.

Flute music off.

EURIPIDES

Phthian A - chilleus as you hear in the slaughter of heroes
oho what a stroke come you not to the rescue?*
Hermes ances - tral, oh how we honor you, we of the lakeside*
oho what a stroke come you not to the rescue?

DIONYSOS

There's two strokes scored against you, Aeschylus.

EURIPIDES

Greatest Achaian, At - reus son who art lord over multitudes hear
me*

oho what a stroke come you not to the
rescue?

DIONYSOS

Another stroke, dear Aeschylus. That makes the third.

EURIPIDES

Quiet, all. O bee-keepers - now open the temple of Artemis nearby*
oho what a stroke come you not to the
rescue?
I am enabled - to sing of the prodigy shown at the way-
side*
oho what a stroke come you not to the
rescue?

DIONYSOS

Oh what a mess of strokes, lord Zeus, I'm on the ropes.
Stroke upon stroke has got my kidneys black and blue.
I think I'd better go and take a soothing bath.

EURIPIDES

Wait till you've listened to my next melodic line-up.
We will now take up the music written for the lyre.

DIONYSOS

Go ahead. But leave the strokes out, will you please.

EURIPIDES

How the twin-throned — power of Achaia and manhood of Hellas*
di tum di tum di tum di tum
Sends forth the — sphinx who is princess of ominous hell-
hounds*
di tum di tum di tum di tum

*hand on the — spear and embattled, the bird of encounter**
        di tum di tum di tum di tum
giving assault — there to the hovering hounds of the air-
    *ways**
        di tum di tum di tum di tum.

DIONYSOS

Where did you get this tum diddy stuff? From Marathon?*
It sounds like water-pulling-from-the-well-up music.

AESCHYLUS

My source is excellent, if that's what you mean, the result
excellent too. I only tried not to be seen
reaping the same Muse-meadow Phrynichos had reaped.
But this man draws from every kind of source, burlesque,
Meletos'* drinking-ditties, all that Karian jazz,
dirges, folksongs. Here, let me show you. Bring me a lyre
somebody. Wait! No, don't. What's the use of a lyre
for this stuff? Where's that girl who uses oyster shells
for castanets? Hither, Euripidean Muse.

A scantily clad girl comes on. Aeschylus bows to her
with mock ceremony.

To thee, onlie begetter of these melodies.

DIONYSOS

So that's the Tenth Muse is it? Well, she ain't no Sappho.
That's a man's woman if I ever saw one.*

AESCHYLUS

*Halycon-birds who in the sea's ever-streaming**
billows twittering
dabble wings in the flying spray
dipping and ducking feathery forms:
you in the angles under the roof
finger-wee-hee-heeving embattled
handiwork of your woof-warp-webs,
singing shuttle's endeavor
where the flute-loving dolphin leaps
next the cutwater's darkened edge
oracular in her pastures,
gleam and joy of the grapevine
where clusters of heart's ease curl and cling.
Circle me in your arms, o my child.

Breaking off in disgust.

Just look at that line.

DIONYSOS

I'm looking.

AESCHYLUS

And look at *that* one.

DIONYSOS

I'm looking.

AESCHYLUS

And you the writer of lines like that
dare to say that my verse is bad.
Yours is made like a whore displayed
in all the amorous postures.

So much for your choral metres. Now I'll demonstrate
the composition of your lyric monodies.*

O darkness of night, shining
in gloom, what vision of dream
bring you poor me
fished from the occult depths,
envoy of Hades
spiritless spirit possessing,
child of the sable night,
ghastly grim apparition
in dark trappings of death
and bloodily bloodily glaring,
and her nails were long they were long.
Help me, my handmaidens, light up the lanterns and
run with your pitchers and fetch from the river and heat up the water
that I may wash this vision from me.

O spirit of the sea
that was it. Heigh-ho housemates
behold, here are portents.
Glyke has stolen my rooster away,
and lo, she is gone.
O ye nymphs of the mountains,
Mania, arrest her.

Soft you now. I was sitting
plying my humble tasks
at the loom filled with its flax
wee-hee-hee-hee-hee-hee-heeving
with my hands, spinning a veil

so I could take it at dawn
to market to market it there,
and he fluttered he fluttered away
on gossamer wings to the air
and sorrows sorrows he left me
and tears tears from my eyes
I shed I shed. Poor me.

But o Kretans, nurselings of Ida,
seize your bows and come to aid me,
prithee, shake your leaping legs and surround me the house,
with you Diktynna, and Artemis—pretty child—
holding her puppies in leash let her search the premises,
and you, Zeus' daughter, in both hands upholding
your brightest twin torches, appear, o Hekate,
at Glyke's house, that I may
get her with the goods. (My ravishéd rooster.)

DIONYSOS
That will be all for the lyric verse.

AESCHYLUS
                                   I've had enough.
I want to bring him out and put him to the scales,
for that alone will show our poetry's true weight.
Weigh phrase with phrase, for their specific gravity.

DIONYSOS
Bring out the scales then, if my duty is to judge
two master poets like a grocer selling cheese.

CHORUS
Devious is the great intellect.
Here is a portent of poetry
beyond what anyone could expect.
Who could have thought of this, but he?
Had anyone else proceeded
to such invention
I would have said he needed
medical attention.

Scales are brought. As each poet speaks one of the
lines of verse, he drops, I think, a scrap of papyrus
into the scale pan.

DIONYSOS
Now take your places by the weighing pans.

AESCHYLUS AND EURIPIDES
                                        Ready.

DIONYSOS
Each of you hold his line while he is speaking it.
Don't drop it in the pan until I say "cuckoo."

AESCHYLUS AND EURIPIDES
We have them.

DIONYSOS
                    Say and lay a line upon the scale.

EURIPIDES
*I wish the Argo's hull had never winged her way.**

AESCHYLUS
*River Spercheios with your cattle-pastures near.**

DIONYSOS
Cuckoo! Let go.
The slips drop, and the scale of Aeschylus descends.
                        Aha. The scale of Aeschylus
is far the heavier.

EURIPIDES
                    What can be the cause of that?

DIONYSOS
He put a river in it, the wool-merchant's trick,
and soaked his words in water as they do their wool.
But you put in a winged word, a feathery line.

EURIPIDES
Have him speak another one. Match us again.

DIONYSOS
Take your next lines.

AESCHYLUS AND EURIPIDES
                    We're ready.

DIONYSOS
                                    Speak them.
Same business as before.

EURIPIDES
*Persuasion has no shrine except within the word.**

AESCHYLUS
*Death is the only god who is not moved by gifts.**

DIONYSOS
Let go, let go. Aeschylus has the weight again.
He put Death in. There's nothing more *depressing* than that.

EURIPIDES
But I put in Persuasion. That's a handsome word.

DIONYSOS
Persuasion she's a scatterbrain, a featherweight.
Better see if you can't turn up a heavier line,
something massive and bulky, that will give you heft.

*Euripides frantically rummages through a pile of
papers, muttering to himself.*

EURIPIDES
Now where on earth did I put my lines like that?

DIONYSOS
                                        Here's one.
"Achilleus threw the dice, and shot a deuce and a four."
All right, ready with your lines. This is the final test.

EURIPIDES
*His right hand seized the spear heavily shod with steel.**

AESCHYLUS
*Chariot piled on chariot and corpse on corpse.**

DIONYSOS
Aeschylus fooled you again.

EURIPIDES
                    How?

DIONYSOS
Threw in a couple of chariots and two dead men.
A hundred Egyptian coolies couldn't lift that load.

AESCHYLUS
Don't do it line by line, now. Let him climb in the scale
with his children and his wife, I mean Kephisophon,
and all his books, and hold them in his lap. I'll speak
only two lines of verse, and still I'll sink the scale.

DIONYSOS

Gentlemen, my friends. I can not judge them any more.
I must not lose the love of either one of them.
One of them's a great poet. I like the other one.

PLUTO

You mean, you won't do what you came down here to do?

DIONYSOS

And if I do decide?

PLUTO

                              Then take the one you want
and go; we must not let your journey be in vain.

DIONYSOS

To Pluto.

Bless your heart.

To the poets.

                              Very well, then. Answer me this.
I came down here to get a poet. Why? To help
our city survive, so it can stage my choruses.
The one of you who has the best advice to give
for saving the city is the one that I'll take back.
Alkibiades is a baby who's giving
our state delivery-pains. What shall we do with him?
That's the first question.

EURIPIDES

                              How does the state feel about him?

DIONYSOS

It longs for him, it hates him, and it wants him back.
Speak your minds both, and tell us what we are to do.

EURIPIDES

I hate the citizen who, by nature well endowed,
is slow to help his city, swift to do her harm,
to himself useful, useless to the community.

DIONYSOS

Good answer, by Poseidon.

To Aeschylus.

                              Now, what about you?

AESCHYLUS

We should not rear a lion's cub within the state.
[Lions are lords. We should not have them here at all.]*
But if we rear one, we must do as it desires.

DIONYSOS

By Zeus the Savior, I still can't make up my mind.
One answer was so clever. The other was so clear.
Give me one more opinion, each of you.
How can we save the city?

EURIPIDES

Give Kleokritos Kinesias* to serve as wings;
let him be airborne over the vast sea's expanse.

DIONYSOS

Well, that would be amusing. Would there be some point?

EURIPIDES

They could be armed with vinegar-jars, and bomb
the enemy at sea with vinegar in their eyes.

Embarrassed pause.

No, really, I do know what to do. Let me speak.

DIONYSOS

                                        Speak.

EURIPIDES

When that we trust not now, we trust, and trust no more
what now we do trust—we shall win.

DIONYSOS

                              How's that again?
Please be a bit more stupid, so I'll understand.

EURIPIDES

If we mistrust those citizens whom now we trust,
and use those citizens whom we do not use now,
we might be saved.
If we are losing using what we use, will it
not follow we might win by doing the opposite?

DIONYSOS

Ingenious, o my Palamedes, soul of wit.
Did you think that up yourself, or was it Kephisophon?

87

EURIPIDES
All by myself. The vinegar was Kephisophon.

DIONYSOS
Well, Aeschylus, what is your view?

AESCHYLUS
                     First tell me this.
Which men *is* Athens using? Her best?

DIONYSOS
                   Her best? Where've *you* been?
She hates them like poison.

AESCHYLUS
           Does she really like her worst men?

DIONYSOS
She doesn't *like* them. Uses them because she has to.

AESCHYLUS
How can you pull a city like that out of the water
when neither the fine mantle nor coarse cloak will serve?*

DIONYSOS
Better find something, or she'll sink and never come up.

AESCHYLUS
I'd rather tell you up there. I don't want to down here.

DIONYSOS
Oh please, yes. Send your blessings up from underground.

AESCHYLUS
They shall win—
when they think of their land as if it were their enemies',
and think of their enemies' land as if it were their own,
that ships are all their wealth, and all their wealth, despair.

DIONYSOS
Good! But the jurymen will eat up all that wealth.

PLUTO
Decide.

DIONYSOS
     Out of their own mouths have they spoken it.
For I shall choose the poet that my soul desires.

EURIPIDES
Do not forget the vows you swore by all the gods,
to take me home with you. Choose him who loves you best.

DIONYSOS
*My tongue swore, not my heart.** I'm taking Aeschylus.

EURIPIDES
Can you do this, and look me in the face for shame?

DIONYSOS
*What's shameful?—unless it seems so to the audience?**

EURIPIDES
And wilt thou leave me thus for dead? Say nay, say nay.

DIONYSOS
*Who knows if life be death indeed or death be life,**
or breath be breakfast, sleep in fleece be comforter?

PLUTO
Go all inside now, Dionysos.

DIONYSOS
                                Why, what for?

PLUTO
So I can feast you before you sail away.

DIONYSOS
                                Good news.
I am not discontented with my morning's work.

CHORUS
Blessed he
who has such wisdom and wit.
Many can learn from it.
Through good counsel he won the right
to return home again
for the good of the cause and state,
for the good of his fellow men,
to help them fight the good fight
with his great brain.

Better not to sit at the feet
of Sokrates* and chatter,
nor cast out of the heart
the high serious matter
of tragic art.
Better not to compete
in the no-good lazy
Sokratic dialogue.
Man, that *is* crazy.

PLUTO
Go forth rejoicing, Aeschylus, go,
save us our city
by your good sense and integrity.
Instruct the foolish majority.
Here is a rope to give Kleophon,
here's one for the revenuers,
Myrmex and Nikomachos,
this for Archenomos,*
tell them their hour
has come; they are waited for here, today,
and if they delay
I, in person, will go brand them, sting them,
sling them each in a thong
and bring them
here to Hades', where they belong.

AESCHYLUS
All this I will do. Here is my Chair
of Tragedy. Give it to Sophocles there
to keep for me until I come down
once more, for I judge him to be
the greatest of poets—after me.
But mind: never give My Chair
over to the vile uses
of this pseudo-poet, this lying clown.
Not even if he refuses.

PLUTO
Torches, this way.
With holy illumination light him
and with his own songs and dances delight him
as you escort him away.

CHORUS

First, o divinities under the ground indwelling, we pray you,
grant fair journey to the poet as he goes back to the daylight:
grant him success in all the thoughts that will prosper our city.
So at last may we find surcease from sorrows we suffer
through war's encounters. Let Kleophon and all similar aliens
who love to fight go home and fight—in the lands of their fathers.

Notes

page 7. *Phrynichos, Lykis, Ameipsias:* Comic poets, rivals of Aristophanes.

8. *sea battle:* The battle of Arginousai, fought in 406 B.C., the summer before this play. Slaves were then used in the Athenian navy for the first time, and these slaves were set free after the victory.

11. *Kleisthenes:* Aristophanes makes him a synonym for effeminacy and homosexuality throughout his plays (see also page 34 in this play) and uses him as a character in *The Thesmophoriazusae.*

11. *Molon:* An actor apparently, who was either very little or very large.

12. *For some . . . are bad:* From the lost *Oeneus* of Euripides.

13. *Iophon:* The son of Sophocles. The point here and in the following lines was that the younger man had been helped by his father.

13. *Agathon:* A tragic poet whose works are lost but who had a good reputation as a poet and seems to have been personally very well liked. There are portraits of him in Plato's *Symposium* and Aristophanes' *Thesmophoriazusae,* and though the latter teases him for a ladylike manner and appearance, the teasing is done without Aristophanes' usual cruelty. The reader would think Agathon had died. He had not. At some time not long before this play, he left Athens and joined a group of celebrities at the court of King Archelaos in Macedonia. The thought is, that for Athenian audiences he might just as well have quitted this world for the Islands of the Blest at the end of the world. Little is known about Xenocles and nothing about Pythangelos.

14. *Bright upper air, Zeus' penthouse:* All these lines are Euripidean. "Bright upper air, Zeus' penthouse" seems to be adapted from a phrase in the lost *Clever Melanippe.* "The foot of Time" is from the lost *Alexander.* The *heart that would . . .* and *Tongue that was . . .* are an adaptation from *Hippolytus* 612.

14. *Rule thou it:* This line is Euripidean, but the scholiast's ascription of it to *Andromache* is wrong.

16. *the deathless way:* As the Greeks conceived it, death is the separation of the soul or *psyche* (life, breath, ghost, or image) from the body. The body decays. The soul, such as it is, goes to the house or realm of Hades, or

to Hades (Hades is Plouton or Pluto, a person rather than a place). Usually, *but not always,* Hades is imagined to be under the ground. An alternate thought is to put the land of the dead, sometimes of the blessed dead only, at the end of the world. So certain special heroes pass to the other world merely by going further than natural means could have taken anyone: they do not go underground, their psyche is not torn out of their body, *they do not die.* Odysseus makes a long voyage and returns. Herakles went, and came back alive, so he must have gone by the roundabout way (Tainaron, land's end of the Peloponnese, the jumping-off place). In *The Metamorphoses* (*The Golden Ass*) of Apuleius (6. 17-18), Psyche must do an errand in Hades and return. She climbs a high tower and is about to jump. But the tower tells her not to, for if her spirit is broken out of her body she will go to the deepest place and never come back. Instead, she should go the long way, via Tainaron. Apuleius wrote in the second century A.D., but he helps to show what Dionysos is here talking about. In this play, the ferryboat on the Styx is combined perhaps with the far-voyaging ship, such a one as carried Odysseus. But one should not go too far in quest of intelligibility, since this is a funny play, not theology.

page 16. *two bits:* Literally, two obols. The *diobelia* or "two-obol payment" was a notorious but mysterious payment, probably some kind of dole, instituted by the demagogue Kleophon.

17. *Theseus:* The Athenian hero also made the trip to Hades and back.

17. *Morsimos:* A tragic poet, great-nephew of Aeschylus.

17. *Kinesias:* A writer of dithyrambs.

17. *Initiates:* Those initiated in the Eleusinian Mysteries expected a blissful life after death.

18. *bucks:* Literally, drachmas.

19. *carry me home:* The Greek here has a punning sequence only a little less idiotic than the translation.

20. *sea battle:* See the note to page 8.

20. *Stone of Parching Thirst:* (*Auainou lithos*). This would be a landmark in the country of the dead. Refreshing *water* from the Well of Memory stands for immortality ("may Isis give you cold water" on many Greek-Egyptian epitaphs): so being dried out would be a preliminary torment.

21. *First Crew:* Literally, "I am asalaminious." This could mean, "I am not a Salamis man," that is "I didn't fight at the battle of Salamis." But it could also mean "I am not a Salaminia man." The "Salaminia" was a consecrated ship, used for sacred and special missions. Its crew would doubtless be picked men. Since the sea fight of seventy-five years earlier is quite remote from this part of the play's action, I prefer the second interpretation.

28. *Empousa:* A bogey to frighten children with.

29. *the clam has stilled the waves:* In Euripides *Orestes* 279 the line runs:

ἐκ κυμάτων γὰρ αὖθις αὖ γαλήν(α) ὁρῶ.

The storm is over and the *calm* has stilled the waves.

But the actor, Hegelochos, spoke it:

ἐκ κυμάτων γὰρ αὖθις αὖ γαλῆν ὁρῶ.

The storm is over and the *cat* has stilled the waves.

Since "cat" (or "weasel"?) makes no plausible confusion in English, I have taken a slight liberty. In this, I find I have been anticipated by Mr. Dudley Fitts.

29. *all in yellow:* This seems the likeliest interpretation, though it is difficult to have the donkey on stage for so long.

30. *Iacchos:* Both Dionysos *and* the companion of Demeter and Persephone (that the god is eavesdropping on his own rituals is part of the fun). In the choral passage to come, and in the parabasis, the features of the Mysteries are combined with the worship of the Muses—which is drama.

30. *Diagoras:* A poet notorious for his atheism.

30. *Roasting pigs!:* Pigs were sacrificed at the Mysteries.

31. *Kratinos:* A distinguished comic poet, older contemporary (no longer living at the time of this play) of Aristophanes.

31. *Thorykion:* A tax-collector, evidently. Nothing is known about him except what is alleged here.

31. *shrine as a backhouse:* This seems to mean Kinesias. See page 17.

33. *Archedemos:* The demagogue who instituted proceedings against the generals after the battle of Arginousai (see the note on page 39). Non-Athenian birth is a frequent charge brought against demagogues by the comic poets.

34. *Kleisthenes:* See page 11. He is supposed to be mourning for a lost boy friend, like a wife for a husband killed in the war. Mourners tore out their hair (from their heads) and beat their faces.

34. *Kallias:* Member of a very rich family in Athens. Then as now only the rich raced horses.

35. *Aiakos:* In epic and saga a great hero, grandfather of Achilleus, head of that heroic line, the Aiakidai, so dear to the Aiginetans and Pindar and, according to some, made for his uprightness a judge of the dead in the underworld. Here he is a slave, plainly the janitor or porter.

35. *Styx, Acheron, Kokytos:* The rivers of the underworld. But Styx, often personified, is here hinted at in her true and ancient form, a waterfall dribbling off a huge black cliff on the northern face of Mount Chelmos, between Arkadia and Achaia.

37. *I cannot but obey thee:* This sounds like a tragic tag, but I cannot place it.

37. *Mistress:* Persephone.

39. *Theramenes:* A well-known politician of the time. Having in mind his own schemes for reform, he would join whatever party seemed temporarily to be most likely to further them, and then change sides at dis-

cretion. He showed the same kind of "adaptability" after the victory at Arginousai (see page 8). Bad weather prevented the victorious Athenians from picking up many survivors and floating corpses after the battle. The assembly was out for blood, and things looked bad for the captains of the ships, of whom Theramenes was one. He saved himself by adding his voice to the clamor, but putting the blame on the admirals of the fleet, who were condemned to death. Such maneuvers won Theramenes the nickname *kothornos,* which means "tragic buskin," or a military boot, or, more important for our purpose here, any boot which would fit either foot. The nickname is attested by Xenophon *Hellenica* 2. 3. 31. It does not appear in our text. I apologize for crowding it in; it seemed to me to make clear the well-known character of the man Aristophanes was attacking.

page 42. *Kleon:* If you have read the early plays, especially *The Knights,* you know all about Kleon. Hyperbolos was his successor, and of the same sort.

43. *my wife:* He hasn't any.

43. *my kiddies:* He hasn't any.

43. *the kind of god:* Herakles, as brother of Dionysos, is treated mostly as a god in this play.

43. *brave herbs:* Oregano. It was supposed to put one in a fighting mood.

44. *gentlemanly:* Athenian law permitted the torture of slaves in order to make them give evidence. This could not be done to free men, or "gentlemen," so it is a "generous" and "gentlemanly" gesture on the part of Xanthias when he offers his *slave* to be tortured for evidence concerning *himself.*

44. *or leeks:* A master might ask that his slave be excused from tortures too injurious or painful, either for the slave's own sake, or with thoughts of his future uses.

47. *Diomeia:* This feast of Herakles was held outside the walls and could not be celebrated while the enemy occupied Attica.

48. *Apollo . . . Pytho:* A line of verse by Hipponax, the iambic poet.

48. *Who . . . green waters:* The lyric is said to be from the lost *Laocoön* of Sophocles.

48. *Kleophon:* Politician, leader of the popular party, which was also the war party, detested by the comic poets, and attacked as being of non-Athenian (Thracian) birth. See the last lines of this play. Swallow and nightingale (Philomela and Prokne) are associated with Thrace (see *The Birds*), and the twittering of birds is often used to describe barbarian speech. The point is apparently something like this: Kleophon must stand trial at some time, and though in Attic law even ballots mean acquittal, Kleophon is so awful that an exception ought to be made.

49. *fears be taken away:* What follows is a plea for amnesty, and the restoration of full citizens' rights to all those who had lost them for political

reasons, particularly for supporting Phrynichos in the revolution of 411 B.C.

page 49. *Plataian status:* Plataia, a city of Boiotia, had been the most steadfast and devoted of the allies of Athens. When in 427 B.C. the city was destroyed by the Spartans and Thebans, the survivors were granted Athenian citizenship (with a few limitations).

49. *Kleigenes:* This bathman was doubtless also a politician, but we know nothing more about him.

49. *currency:* The Spartan occupation of part of Attica had cut off access to the silver mines at Laurion. This resulted in a debasing of the coinage.

50. *scapegoat:* Or *pharmakos.* This was a condemned criminal on whom was loaded all the accumulated guilt of the city. His execution, therefore, amounted to an act of public sacrifice and expiation.

53. *Kleidemidas:* Perhaps a son of Sophocles, perhaps only a friend.

55. *cabbage patch:* Aristophanes is fond of saying that Euripides' mother maintained a truck garden.

59. *Phrynichus:* The earliest of the great tragic poets, active in the first decades of the fifth century (not to be confused with the comic poet mentioned on page 7).

59. *Achilleus:* References are to lost plays, *The Phrygians* (or *The Ransoming of Hector*) and *Niobe.*

61. *Kephisophon:* Euripides' secretary, supposed, here, to have done some ghostwriting for him.

61. *line of thought:* Aristophanes portrays Aeschylus as a haughty patrician who disliked the common people. See the Introduction.

62. *Phormisios:* A "reactionary" politician. Of Megainetos and Manes (this may be a nickname) nothing is known. Kleitophon, who appears in the dialogue of Plato which bears his name, seems to have belonged with Phormisios, as does Theramenes (see note 39 on page 95). Euripides' disciples seem to be distinguished from those of Aeschylus not so much for their views as for their characters and methods.

63. *See you . . . Achilleus?:* The opening of the lost *Myrmidons* of Aeschylus.

65. *Persians:* This seems to be a slip of memory on the part of Aristophanes. *The Persians* is reliably dated 472 B.C., *The Seven Against Thebes* 467 B.C.

66. *Phaidra:* See Euripides, *Hippolytus.*

66. *Sthenoboia:* The heroine of a lost play named after her. Her story is similar to that of Phaidra, insofar as she made advances to Bellerophon, her husband's guest, was refused, and told her husband that Bellerophon had tried to seduce her.

68. *warships:* No one is willing to be a *trierarch.* The *trierarchy,* a special duty or liturgy imposed on rich citizens, involved the outfitting and upkeep of a *trireme* (war galley), as well as the nominal command of the vessel on active service.

69. *His nurses . . . life?:* The nurse-procuress could be Phaidra's nurse in

Hippolytus. In *Auge,* the heroine gave birth in the temple of Athene. In *Aeolus,* Makareus and Kanake, brother and sister, are involved in a love affair. For musings on life, see the fragment from the lost *Polyeidus:*

> Who knows if life be not thought death, or death be life in the world below?

There is a similar thought in the lost *Phrixus.*

page 69. *Panathenaia:* The pan-Athenian festival.

70. *subtle allusions:* We are told that *The Frogs* was so well received that a second performance was given during the poet's lifetime. This stanza may conceivably have been written for this second performance, when "the book was out." But an annotated edition, by which the audience could identify allusions, is something absolutely unexampled for this date.

70. *Oresteia:* The title is here used for the play we call *The Choephori,* or *The Libation Bearers.*

71. *Hermes, . . . I have returned:* These lines are missing from our mss. of Aeschylus. I have discarded my previous translation for a more literal one, in order to make the use of synonymous phrases, real or apparent, more obvious.

73. *three times:* At the last rites for the dead, the name was called three times.

74. *Oedipus . . . man:* This and the fifth line below are the first two lines of Euripides' lost *Antigone.*

74. *Erasinides:* A general at the time of the battle of Arginousai. Had one of these generals lost his sight, he would have been excused from military service, and so would have escaped the fate that befell Erasinides and his colleagues. See the note on Theramenes on page 95.

75. *Aigyptos . . . Argos:* Said to have been the first lines of the lost *Archelaus,* but the opening of this play is also given in another form.

75. *little bottle of oil:* The *lekythion,* or little oil bottle, was part of the traveler's regular luggage.

75. *Dionysos . . . feet:* Opening of the lost *Hypsipyle.*

75. *Ah me, . . . again:* This line combines the two death cries of Agamemnon, Aeschylus *Agamemnon* 1343, 1345.

75. *There's been . . . born unhappy:* Opening of the lost *Sthenoboea.*

76. *Kadmos . . . Sidon:* Opening of the lost *Phrixus.*

76. *Pelops . . . horses:* Opening of *Iphigeneia in Tauris.*

77. *Oineus, from his land:* Opening of the lost *Meleager.*

77. *Zeus . . . maintained:* Opening of the lost *Clever Melanippe.*

78. *Phthian . . . rescue?:* Two lines from the lost *Myrmidons,* the second repeated as a refrain by Aristophanes.

78. *Hermes . . . lakeside:* From the lost *Psychagogi.*

78. *Greatest Achaian . . . hear me:* From either *Telephus* or *Iphigeneia* (both lost).

78. *Quiet, all . . . nearby:* From *The Priestesses* (lost).

78. *I am . . . at the wayside: Agamemnon* 104.

78. *How the . . . of Hellas: Agamemnon* 108.

78. *Sends forth . . . hellhounds:* From the lost *Sphinx.*

79. *hand on . . . of encounter: Agamemnon* 111.

79. *giving assault . . . airways:* Provenance unknown.

79. *From Marathon:* The next Aeschylean line, *which leaning on Aias,* is meaningless here, since unmetrical, and I have omitted it.

79. *Meletos':* A poet of indifferent reputation, better known as the accuser of Socrates.

79. *That's a man's woman . . . one:* Literally, Dionysos says: "This Muse was never a Lesbian, not at all." Rogers, reading the Greek so as to obtain "The Muse herself" instead of "This Muse," translates: "The Muse herself can't be a wanton? No!" I do not find this convincing. Outraged indignation does not suit Dionysos, and the expression "be a Lesbian" should not mean "be a wanton" in any general sense. If Sappho had ever, at this time, been called "The tenth Muse," the point would be perfect. She was so called, but I do not find it earlier than *Palatine Anthology* 9. 506. This is attributed to Plato, and therefore could, by an exceedingly strenuous stretch of the imagination, have been current before *The Frogs* was written. But attributions in the *Anthology* are frequently suspect, and this epigram does not sound Platonic to me. Still, "Tenth Muse" could have been a tag already applied to Sappho, and the allusion to Lesbos ought to be accounted for in the translation.

79. *sea's ever-streaming:* This sequence seems to be a patchwork of Euripidean passages, but not all can be identified. The first four lines are said to be from *Iphigeneia,* but do not appear in our extant texts for either of the plays so called. Other identifications are: the eighth line, *Meleager;* ninth and tenth, *Electra;* eleventh to fourteenth, *Hypsipyle.*

81. *monodies:* The monody is a solo for the female character (played of course by a male actor). Unlike the patchwork demonstration of "Euripidean lyric" above, this is a true parody, done "in the manner of Euripides" but without (apparently) direct quotations.

83. *I wish . . . her way:* The opening line of *Medea.*

83. *River . . . near:* From the lost *Philoctetes.*

83. *Persuasion . . . the word:* From the lost *Antigone.*

85. *Death . . . by gifts:* From the lost *Niobe.*

85. *His right hand . . . steel:* From the lost *Meleager.*

85. *Chariot . . . on corpse:* From the lost *Glaucus.*

87. *[Lions . . . all]:* The authenticity of this line, omitted by two good mss., is highly doubtful, so I have left it in square brackets. The allusion to the lion's cub may be to *Agamemnon* 716-36, but there is no direct quotation. Lions are constantly associated with kingship. There would be a hint at Alkibiades' suspected ambitions toward tyranny. I have read this thought into my translation. To the question, what shall we do about Alkibiades, the answers may be paraphrased thus: Euripides: He is

selfish and therefore unreliable: Aeschylus: True, but he is our only promising leader, and we should put ourselves in his hands.

page 87. *Kleokritos* and *Kinesias:* see *The Birds* 877, 1372.

88. *will serve?:* I hope I am right in this interpretation. Neither the mantle of the rich nor the sackcloth of the poor is satisfactory. These articles of clothing are, I believe, thought of as emergency life preservers. Cp. *Odyssey* 5. 346-50.

89. *My tongue . . . heart:* See *Hippolytus* 612.

89. *What's shameful? . . . audience?:* Adapted from the lost *Aeolus.* It should read: "What's shameful, unless it seems so to those who do it?"

89. *Who knows . . . life:* See note 69 on page 97.

90. *Sokrates:* The word *sophia* stands sometimes for literary skill, sometimes for wisdom. The ambiguity shows that the Greeks did not always distinguish between the two as sharply as we do. Aristophanes, acknowledging perhaps that the clever Sokrates does possess some kind of *sophia,* rejects it as the wrong kind. The objection is based, clearly, on certain antiliterary views of Sokrates which are attested again and again in the works of Plato.

90. *Archenomos:* They were involved in the collection of taxes.